SELFHOOD & SERVICE; THE RELATION OF CHRISTIAN PERSONALITY TO WEALTH & SOCIAL REDEMPTION

Published @ 2017 Trieste Publishing Pty Ltd

ISBN 9780649701551

Selfhood & Service; The Relation of Christian Personality to Wealth & Social Redemption by David Beaton

Edited by Trieste Publishing Pty Ltd.
 Cover @ 2017

www.triestepublishing.com

DAVID BEATON

SELFHOOD & SERVICE; THE RELATION OF CHRISTIAN PERSONALITY TO WEALTH & SOCIAL REDEMPTION

Trieste

SELFHOOD AND SERVICE.

SELFHOOD AND SERVICE

THE RELATION OF CHRISTIAN PERSONALITY
TO WEALTH AND SOCIAL REDEMPTION

BY

DAVID BEATON

CHICAGO: NEW YORK: TORONTO

FLEMING H. REVELL COMPANY

1898

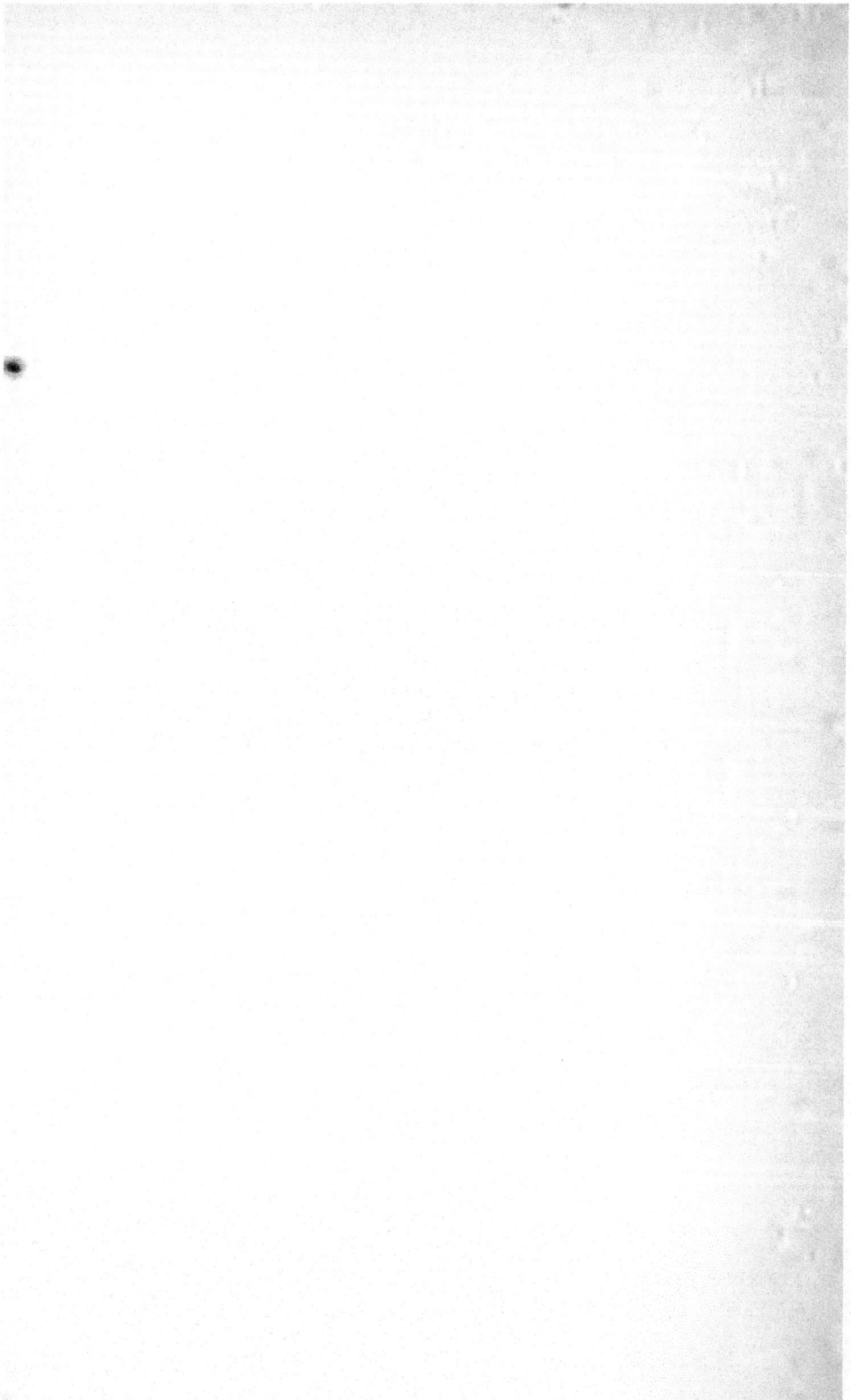

FOREWORD.

It is hoped there is a message in these pages interesting alike to the man of faith and the man of science, more interesting where the two are combined. The motive of the writing is a deep sympathy with the weak, who are forced to the wall in the awful industrial contest of life—the defective, the dispossessed in our present social chaos. The strong need no friends, they can fight their own battles, but the Christian may well say, "Let my tongue cleave to the roof of my mouth, and let my arm wither, when the one shall cease to plead the cause of the poor or the other refuse to defend him." But the facts of Christian history and the stern laws of life must be regarded. A permanent social order can come only from a constructive principle which regards those facts and measures those laws. This principle is set forth here, at once consistent with the claims of personality and the work of social redemption.

DAVID BEATON.

CHICAGO, January, 1898.

7

CONTENTS.

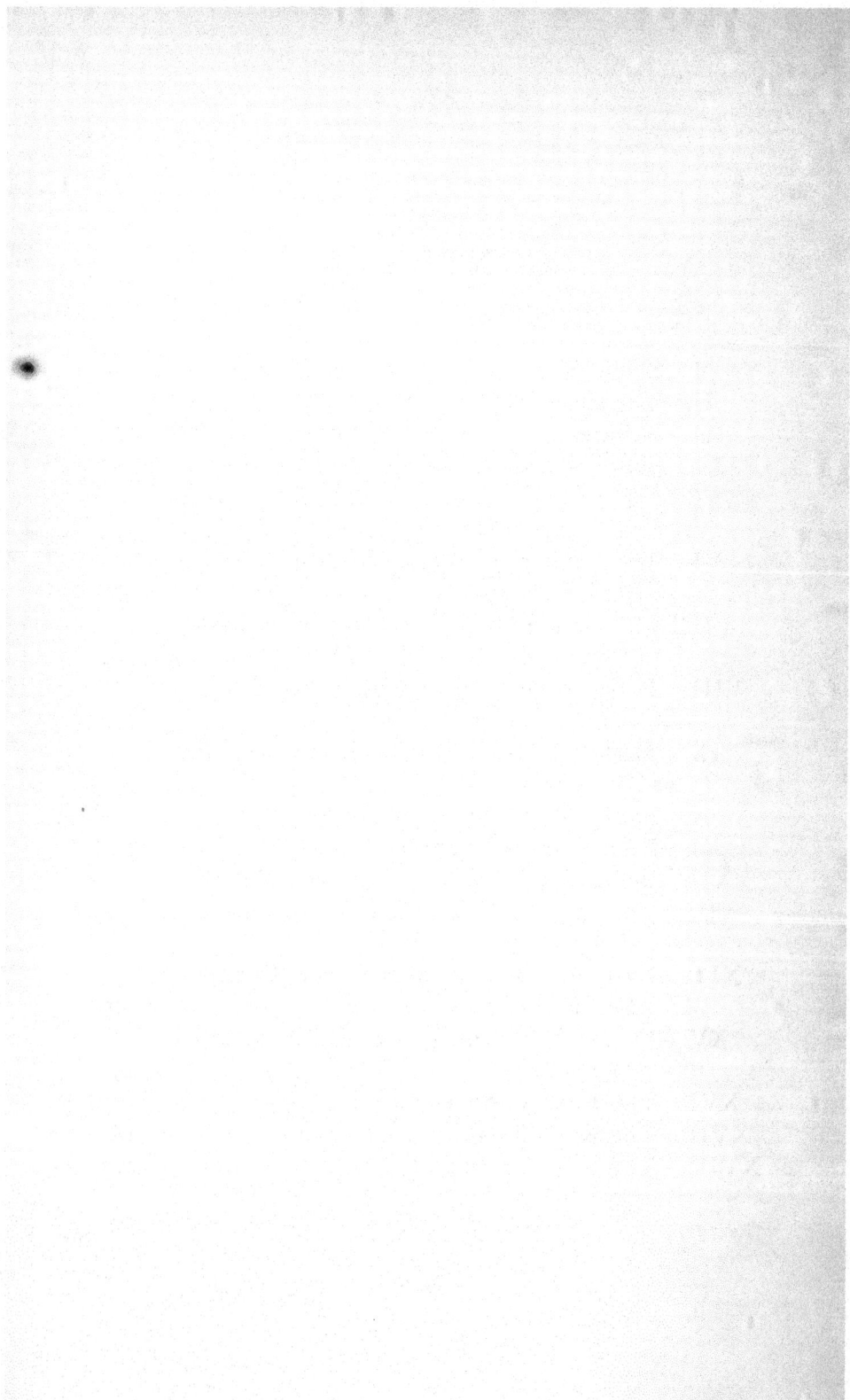

SELFHOOD AND SERVICE.

I.

SOCIAL REDEMPTION THROUGH CHRISTIANITY.

Our age is restless and critical. Christianity has borne the chief brunt of this insurgent spirit. Reformers have been impatient with the church, and said their hardest things against Christians. Many regard this criticism as a sign of enmity to religion, and see in it the birth of a new movement of social reform which casts aside the Christian faith and the guidance of the Christian church. More careful observation of the thought of our time will, however, lead us to quite an opposite conclusion.

Why do the earnest thoughtful men and women, like the majority of our workers in the cause of social redemption, criticise any institution like the church? Just because it professes to be able to cure the ills of human society which they are interested in healing. They do not criticise athletic associations, nor literary societies because these are not called into existence for the moral and social redemption of society. But this is one of the main purposes for which the church exists, and in the accomplishment of which Christianity achieves her most splendid victories.

The social reformer is impatient with the methods of the church because in the depth of his heart he regards her as the right arm of the Lord for the social redemption of man.

Certainly the most touching, as it is also the most reassuring, note of the spirit of our age, is the desire, breaking out into a beseeching, on the part of all social workers, that the church should rouse herself from her indifference to the social needs of the people, and come forth to-day, as in the early days of her poverty and self-denial, renewing her mighty youth in the splendid self abandonment of the Apostles and the early disciples, for the divine ideal of social righteousness and the prosperity of the common people. Indeed a very large part of this severe criticism has come from the best friends of Christianity. To them, the weaknesses and failures of the church as an instrument of social redemption are the signs of a deeper degeneracy in her life, and a more fatal departure from the spirit of her Founder than is to be seen in the partial failure of her work in any one particular direction.

This condition is regarded by them as evidence of a change of ideal and purpose; as a fatal conformity to the world, both in spirit and practice. We know that the first Christians won their triumphs over the heathen world by the virtues born of poverty, by the heroic qualities of peoples inspired by noble ideals, by self-abnegation, contempt of suffering, and disregard of death. They counted not their lives dear unto them for the love of Christ.

They may have made mistakes in their doctrines of political economy, but a new spirit was born into the world, clear-eyed, tender-hearted, yet masterful and splendid in purpose, which changed the face of society and brought liberty, purity, peace, and prosperity to the enslaved and wretched of every race, where the gospel was preached. In marked contrast to this poverty the church is now rich, beside this self-denial the modern Christian is luxurious, and compared with these conquering virtues of self-abnegation and heroism for great ideals, we have prudence and worldly wisdom. And the world sees the sworn soldiers of the cross thankful if they can secure their own ease and preserve their own privileges, letting society and its wrongs cautiously alone.

Has then, the modern Christian church completed the cycle of degeneracy which all conquerors must tread? First, the poor but strong man, hardy, vigorous, eager for conquest, inspired by loyalty or splendid race traditions, seeking the rich and fertile lands of the south, he conquers them by virtue of the physical and mental prowess created by poverty and lofty ideals. Then the possessor, luxurious, cultured, self-indulgent, wise in the conservative maxims of letting things alone, indifferent to high ideals, and in his turn, the helpless prey, as well as the rich prize which tempts the invader.

The business customs and social ideals of many modern Christians give far too much ground for the assertion that such a fatal cycle of degeneracy has been completed by the church of Christ in her nineteen hundred years of history. And if this charge is really proved against the church, no class of workers and thinkers will more deeply lament the fact than those who long for a purified and prosperous social life. The patriot who hailed, in the robust manliness of the first Christian's faith, the promise of a new type of manhood and a new order of citizenship laments it. The social reformer and thinker who saw, in the new doctrines of a common brotherhood for all men, the creative forces of a new society is in despair. But the Christian who looked to that faith and that spirit of brotherhood, not only for a new manhood, a new citizenship, and a new social order, but a divine energy to re-generate the human soul and so re-create society from the heart outward, sees the door of this larger hope shut in his face.

The Christian believer has the deepest interest in this modern controversy; for it is vital to his faith. Is the church recreant to her trust? Is she false to the spirit and purpose of her Founder? Are her ideals to-day directly opposed to those of the first Christians? Has she failed to understand or been powerless to carry out the commands of her Divine Master? Is it true that the practices and ideals of the great mass of His professed followers are rather pagan than Christian? Has the church, by this conformity, to worldly ideals of life, lost those healing and regenerating energies, which alone make her the savior of men and society?

The charges, which both her enemies and friends have brought against the church, are almost entirely connected with her doctrine and practices regarding wealth. Coming into existence as a spiritual force, and at the behest of a spiritual leader, Christianity soon became a power in temporal affairs and a producer of material as well as spiritual blessings for her followers. It is a notorious fact that the vast preponderance of material wealth created during the past fifty years is owned by the professed followers of Jesus Christ.

At present the writer is building no doctrine on this industrial fact; he simply wishes it to be strongly impressed upon the mind of the reader. It is well for us, also, to confine ourselves to the latter half of the present century for definiteness of illustration, because of the unprecedented increase in wealth which has taken place during that period from the scientific discoveries and mechanical improvements of the age.

It does not concern our subject to discuss here whether the methods, by which this wealth has been accumulated, have been wrong economically or morally. It is simply laid down as a fact, vitally related to the work of the church in the world, that her members own and control the vast and unprecedented accumulations of modern wealth both in Europe and America. Not only is wealth thus accumulated, but it is being concentrated in these latter days in vast fortunes in the hands of a few individuals and families. Thomas G. Sherman estimates the wealth of America as ninety-five thousand millions of dollars. His figures concerning the concentration of this wealth have not been seriously disputed. In 1889 he showed that forty-five thousand persons owned more than half of all the wealth of America. On the basis of the tax returns 182 families owned $43,000,000,000, 1,200,000 families owned $7,000,000,000, and 11,620,-000 families owned $11,215,000,000 of the national wealth.

These startling figures are not set down here for a discussion of the economic and legislative questions that arise out of them; but to place before the reader some of the facts of modern social and industrial life that arouse the interest of the Christian socialist, as well as the alarm of the patriot.

Here then, are two circumstances closely related, both in the popular mind, and in the thought of educated social workers. First, that the vast accumulations of wealth in modern times are in the possession of Christian people, and second that this wealth is being steadily and even rapidly concentrated in a few families. In startling contrast to this is the continued hardship, suffering and perplexity of a vast mass of the people. Sir Robert Peel said many years ago that the condition of the laboring man was a dis-

grace and danger to our civilization. "There
is too much suffering and too much perplexity
in his lot; it is absolutely necessary that we
should render the conditions of the manual
laborer less hard and less precarious." Since
those words were spoken by the great representative of the best in the old aristocracy of
England many revolutions in politics, economics, and social conditions have taken place;
and the greater number of them have been directly aimed at improving the lot of the laboring man.

It is hardly an exaggeration to say that the
most splendid achievements of reform during
the past sixty years have been almost entirely
in the interests of the middle and working
classes. The material benefits resulting from
the discoveries of science and the improvements in machinery have accrued almost
entirely to the benefit of those same classes.
Indeed the fame of the great men and women
of the same period has largely been derived
from measures passed in the interest of, and
works done for, the laboring classes. This only
shows how deep was the ditch out of which
the laborer had to be dug. It reveals his
former moral and social degradation, when we
reflect how much was required to be done to
make the life of the manual worker endurable

and worth living. Society could not have existed in the old forms for fifty years longer,
except for those measures of industrial reform,
and social amelioration. But statesmen and
reformers found that they had only scratched
the surface. Lower deeps of misery and want
were brought to light imperatively demanding
relief.

There are vast areas of population both in
Europe and America as degraded, oppressed,
and hopelessly miserable as the classes who
were the shame and terror of England during
the corn-law hunger and chartist riots.

Besides all this, the common people are being
rapidly educated. They know that they are poor
in the midst of plenty, miserable in the midst
of joy, and yet are in possession of political
power which they have been taught to regard
as the doorway to prosperity. The revela-
tions of Booth and Riis and many others concerning the life of the very poor in our large
cities, are alone grave indictments against
modern governments and the church.

The vices, miseries, and sorrows of the submerged classes remain therefore a just charge
against modern Christianity. Simply because
the church of Christ exists for the purpose of
abolishing those evils and healing those sorrows.
She is accepted by the world at her own ap-

praisement.   For this end she was born into
the world.   This is the source of her power
and her honor.   She could furnish no stronger
evidence of her own degeneracy from the spirit
and purpose of her Master than resentment
of this criticism and refusal to hear this trum-
pet call to her highest duty.

II.

THE CHRISTIAN DOCTRINE OF SELFHOOD.

It should occasion no surprise that the accumulation and use of wealth by Christians are made the tests of genuine Christianity by social reformers, because these subjects are vitally related to the particular interests which they have at heart. To them this is real and concrete Christianity. With them social betterment is inseparably connected with the possession of wealth, its absence is invariably connected with social degradation and misery. Material prosperity is, and that justly, their test of social improvement. Christianity itself has taught them this much, as we shall presently see.

It is small wonder then that schemes of social betterment take the form of appeals to Christians to surrender possession, or to restrict accumulation, or distribute their capital among the less fortunate members of society. Jesus had not where to lay his head, Paul was poor, the early Christians were poor; Christians to-day, if they would be like their Mas-

ter, must be poor ;—such is the reasoning, open
or implied, in many of the plans of the Socialist for the regeneration of society.

Christians, by virtue of their wealth and culture, are now members of the privileged classes,
and use their money and influence for selfish ends, and on the side of the world-power,
instead of assisting the cause of the poor and
for social justice and equal industrial opportunity.   Such is the arraignment of the modern
Christian by the social reformer.

Society demands a new sacrifice by the
church, as proof of her power to save. The poverty, the grinding toil, the want of work to
the willing hands that make a bitter chance
of the poor man's lot, the inequality and
injustice in the distribution of the fruits of
his toil, and the thousand social and economic
evils that render the condition of the poor in-
tolerable in modern society, all demand of the
disciples of Jesus Christ healing and removal.

In those very necessities of life where the
victims of our present social order are weak,
the Christian is strong, where he is ignorant
the Christian is wise, where he is an outcast,
and dispossessed, the Christian is a son of privilege and heir of all the glories of our Christian civilization. It is thus seriously maintained that the possession of these privileges

which wealth and culture bring in the course of the ages have changed the spirit and purpose of the church, and that she is no longer the protector of the weak and redresser of the wrongs of the oppressed. That she uses her wealth mainly for the self-indulgent luxury of her own members and to maintain and perpetuate the privileges of a class. That, in a word, there is complete conformity to the world in the spirit and practice of the church to-day. That there is no perceptible difference in politics, business, or social ambitions between the Christian professor and the man of the world.

So that self-interest, self-indulgence, self-culture, self-glory, are the ruling instincts of both alike. This is clearly demonstrated, it is maintained, in the eagerness of both for the accumulation of wealth and the selfishness common to both in its expenditure. There is only one way to cure this disease of worldly conformity among Christians; and that is to return to the poverty, the equality, and purity of early Christianity. There is only one way for the church to become again the champion of the weak and dispossessed, and that is for Christians to surrender their privileges in the interests of industrial equality and social brotherhood.

Brothers, it is said, must be equal, not only in nature, but in opportunity, not only in honor, but in possessions. It is a practical denial of brotherhood for the Christian to possess and enjoy when his social brother is in want and suffering. The Christian has no right to superabundance when his social brother is in want.

Personal property over which the Christian claims the right of absolute enjoyment and control is a violation of the fundamental idea of Christian brotherhood. It is the source of the social inequalities and injustices of the present shameful condition of modern society. While it obtains in the church, she is false to the spirit of her Master and helpless to accomplish the noble work of social redemption. Such are the candid and extreme views of many who love the church and believe in Jesus Christ as the savior of society.

To the sympathetic Christian man, moved by the spirit of Jesus, there is a marvellous fascination in the thought of a condition of society where all the brethren are equal in honor and opportunity and possessed of a common measure of prosperity. It appeals alike to the poetic sentiments, and to the pious aspirations of the Christian heart. What could be more in accordance with the

divine purpose, it would seem, than the removal of all financial and social inequalities
among the social brotherhood? What more
favorable to a holy life than the removal of all
temptations of the spirit by the suppression of
personal ambitions and the adoption of a
happy equality in the material, intellectual, and
moral heritage of the Kingdom of God?

If, however, we may safely judge concerning God's purpose from His action, it is man-
ifestly certain that equality either in gifts,
graces, or material possessions, never was a
part of his plan, in bringing in the Kingdom.
If we are to learn anything from Nature as
well as history on this point, then the one
fact of life, graven deep upon the rocks,
painted on all her blossoms, and dyed into her
noblest life blood, is the existence of inequality—inequality of faculties, of opportunity,
and of character. But out of this inequality
springs her infinite variety, marvellous richness,
and unfailing resource. And Revelation tells
the same story—nowhere common powers and
possessions, but everywhere inequality, variety, and ceaseless struggles to obtain personal
possessions out of which come the divinest
fruits of the spiritual life.

Much as the Christian idealist could wish
to see realized these lofty dreams of social

equality and common possessions for the brotherhood, the stern realities of our mundane life
compel our thoughts to the more prosaic facts
about bread and butter.   What stands in the
way of a common prosperity is not the un-
willingness of the Christian to share his wealth
and surrender his privileges, but the laws of
nature which govern the production of wealth
and the laws of the soul which create personal superiority.

The conditions which nature has exacted as
the price of human prosperity are stern, difficult, and entirely imcompatible with ease, in-
competence, and Utopian dreams of equality.
All schemes, therefore, that involve restriction
of powers, surrender of privileges, limitations
of accumulated wealth, and the renunciation
of the heritage of education and culture on the
part of individual Christians, would be unnatural expedients, doomed to disaster by the
inexorable laws of the physical and mental life
under which we exist.

It follows that even if it could be shown
that the limitation of accumulated wealth
and surrender of social privileges on the part
of Christians would bring back the pristine
purity and noble ideals of the early Christian church, the inalienable rights of Christian personality would still have to be con-

sidered. It is no light matter, even when considered in the interests of social redemption, to ask the Christian to surrender the principle of private property. Christianity appealed to him at first as to a person. His individual nature, with all his varied qualities of head and heart, all his heritage of race and personal experiences, were involved in the fact of his soul's surrender to Jesus Christ.

It was no blunder when the first converts to Christianity, like Paul, laid emphatic stress upon selfhood. He gave a ringing, fearless, enunciation of the doctrine of individuality. One soul was worth worlds.

Christ and the redeemed individual were made to stand out, related to each other, but in splendid isolation from all the rest of the world. The doctrine was fundamental. It involved all the characteristic ideas of Christianity concerning the personality of God and of the regenerated soul, and had in it the promise and potency of a regenerated society.

All remedies for the diseases of society must sacredly respect this doctrine of selfhood. The Christian man owes no obligation to society which would violate the sacred rights of his own manhood. Selfhood is the grand initiative in morals as well as in economics. It is the creator of all intellectual and spiritual, as well as all material wealth. Christian selfhood is therefore a force to be understood and controlled for useful ends, not vilified and destroyed.

Amiel says: "Two tendencies of our epoch are materialism and socialism—each of them ignoring the true value of the human personality, and drowning it in the totality of nature and society." Christianity must resist both those tendencies, socialism as much as materialism; for the one that overwhelms personality quenches the vital spark of religion.

It may be candidly admitted that Christianity has over-emphasized the principle of selfhood, and it has become largely egoism in modern church life. The immense strides made by the present generation in the study of social conditions, make the egoism of Christians a glaring inconsistency, a spiritual anachronism hardly to be tolerated by earnest souls. But we must not tear down the house because the thatch needs mending. Before we consent to the social and spiritual revolution implied in Christian socialism, we must hear what the individual Christian has to say for himself. We must ask what the doctrine of individuality has done for the man and society. For it may be found that the hope of society

even, lies in a redeemed, enriched individuality; and, in the homely language of the nurs-
ery, our over-eager reformers may be in danger of killing the goose that lays the golden
eggs.

III.

SELFHOOD, THE CREATOR OF MATERIAL WEALTH.

When Christianity comes to the individual soul it brings the promise of an abundant life. The Christian writers had to create new words to express the new ideas of their gospel of personal endowment. The language of paganism was too poor to furnish expressions, as its religion and philosophy were too poor to furnish ideas for the new doctrine of a redeemed and enriched personality. The believer in Christ was called into life, grace, virtue, freedom, honor, glory. He was made priest and king; and his submission to Christ as slave in the new Kingdom only emphasized more strikingly his freedom from all servitude of body or mind towards the former tyrants of altar or throne. The pagan mind of the age was dazed with the new ideas of personality. He himself had deified his emperors, but this new faith now deified his slaves. The common attributes of the Christian man gave a more exalted conception of human life than the prerogative of kings.

Is it any wonder that the literature of primitive Christianity contains so many of the boldest and most masterful expressions of individualism? Is it any wonder that historical Christianity has made its mark in the world mainly by means of this characteristic? Nay, we may go farther, and ask, Is it any wonder that its very weaknesses arise from the over-emphasis of this splendid feature of its life?

No one who has any knowledge of the early history of the Gospel, will deny that this doctrine of a redeemed, noble, rich, personal life, was the re-creator of modern European society. Out of that corrupt, hopeless, and powerless pagan world a new life sprang, armed for conquest, with a strong arm, a clear brain, and a tender heart. It was seen, not only in the moral purity and sweet contentment of the individual life, but in the creative energies which affected trade, politics, art, literature, and statesmanship.

Although Christian Selfhood took many years to mould society, its effects upon the individual were instant and decisive. For all individuals called out of the pagan life by the Gospel the results were the same as on the demoniac healed by Jesus, whose friends saw him sitting clothed and in his right mind.

This new life, this Christian selfhood, had its natural instincts, and the laws of its future growth as surely implanted by its divine author as the original physical and mental laws of nature. These instincts at once asserted themselves; these laws went instantly into operation. The instinct of self-preservation is not more imperative on all living things than the primal command of the Gospel, "Grow in grace," "Give heed to thyself," "Hold fast the liberty wherewith Christ hath made you free." The Christian's first duty is to himself. It includes his own soul's salvation, growth, and enrichment; his own education, the development of all his own powers of head and heart, hand, eye, brain, and tongue.

Whenever the early Christian looked over the record of God's dealings with the church in the Old Testament, he saw that the great and wise leaders set forth for his admiration and imitation were men and women of such large, rich, highly-endowed lives. Abraham, the prince and wealthy man of his age; David, Isaiah, Daniel, Deborah, Ruth, Esther were all of them either princes, poets, statesmen, or people of wealth and consequence. When the doings of early Christianity took form in a book, the Christian of the Middle Ages saw, and we of modern times see the same general fact only slightly modified by the circumstances of early Gospel times. Paul was the first scholar of his time, and not only an orator but a highly endowed personality. If Peter and John were fishermen, and, in contrast to the academic education of Paul, were unlearned and ignorant men, they were as intelligent as the average Greek citizen who judged poems and orations, and voted in the council of his nation though he could not write his name. Apollos was a learned and accomplished rhetorician, Luke was a physician, and Lydia of Thyatira was a rich purple merchant.

Christians very soon discovered that to know the traditions of their faith and understand the literature of their sacred books was a liberal education in itself. And to become partakers in the high thoughts and noble works of its great missionaries was to raise one's self to eminence in the leadership of the race. A doctrine of poverty and self-limitation to such a faith is a gross absurdity and contradiction in terms. Expansion, liberty, endowment, physical, mental, and spiritual, were the primal instincts of the new faith, and the only legitimate outcome of its new laws of life.

As its doctrines of faith and repentance had purified the heart and spirit of man, so its

ideals of personal excellence inevitably tended to adorn and enrich every phase of his
physical and mental life. Christianity has the
promise of the life that now is, as well as the
life to come. Such a statement can have no
meaning unless it includes the discipline and
culture of all our powers of body and mind
and spirit, and carries with it the fruits of honest industry and enlightened enterprise as a
personal possession. Poverty is no pet doctrine of Christianity. There is no recorded
beatitude for the pauper. Poverty restricts
the natural faculties and represses the aspirations of the Christian spirit.

The social ideal of Christianity does not con-
template a condition of tame mediocrity. Of
the poor the poet has said

> Chill penury repressed their noble rage
> And froze the genial current of the soul.

That is good religion as well as good poetry.
The *res angusta domi*, the harrow of poverty,
has gone deep into many a soul. It sours
without humbling the spirit. The servile
vices of slavery are not more contrary to the
spirit of Christianity than the vices of pauperism.

Conformity to worldly ideals, desire for the
larger life, its pleasures and ambitions, are
not by any means absent from the breast of

the poor man. Indeed, there are some forms of worldliness that are more deeply intensified by poverty than by the possession of wealth. The bitterest quarrels over wills occur most frequently where the inheritance is small and the heirs are poor. There is, on the contrary, a certain contempt of what the world can give, a certain lofty scorn of its pretensions, possible only to the man who has always lived in afflu-ence.

The error in Christian history which made the ascetic and anchorite fashionable, which drove half the church into monasteries and convents, would be repeated in essence in our own day should we restrict the possession of wealth in an attempt to clarify the spirit of worldliness. The outcome of the previous ef-forts was greater luxury, pride, and conformity than the world has ever seen. To-day the richest community on earth is one whose fundamental vow is poverty. We cannot control the re-sistless energies of the human spirit by an external rule so rude as the restriction of its material possessions.

Christianity during the ages may have made many mistakes in the use of those individual powers, so brought into exercise, in its asser-tion of social privileges and its expenditure of wealth, but they cannot be corrected by schemes of socialism and confiscation, which contradict and belie the essential promises and hopes of the Gospel.

No page of human history is more splendidly beneficent than that which records the story of Christianity's redemption and enrichment of individual lives; and the eye must be blind indeed which fails to see that material prosperity, freedom, and culture of the individual, the home, and society itself come in the train of this spiritual regeneration of the individual soul.

But the full force of this principle of individual enrichment cannot be fully felt until we examine its effects upon family life. The family is in reality, a part of the individual. His truest, noblest individuality grows out of and returns into the family. It is the true integer and norm of society; and when the Christian religion touches a man's life, its deepest and most lasting benefits reach quickly down into the secret springs of family life.

Personally the believer becomes intelligent, industrious, and ambitious of attaining all intellectual and social advantages which the new life offers him. Physically, as well as morally, he is a new creature. His environment, as well as his heart, is changed.

He now becomes an important factor in the

production of wealth ; most likely a more skilled workman, certainly a more reliable and conscientious one. He is more careful of his material possessions, more thrifty, while at the same time he consumes, for his own proper purposes, more and better articles of food and clothing.

He is also an important consideration in the element of supply and demand affecting the markets of the world. His very ideals at once tend to clothe themselves in concrete facts. They have created new wants, so that the regenerative forces of Christianity in one generation tell upon the wealth of the world and the current prices of the market.

Nay, they reach further—even affecting the plans and ambitions of his life. His new notions of life are seen, not only at his table and his recreations, but in his thinking and education.

Yet, great as these effects are, they become insignificant compared with the vital changes which affect his family. In the individual there may be instances in which these changes are but slightly apparent. In the families of a generation or two they produce a revolution.

In relation to the future career of his children the Christian man is not only a new creature, but a new social force. Socially he is the creator of Christian states, and of modern civilized society.

It is much for Christianity to have been the conqueror of the leading intellects of ancient and modern Europe and America, but that circumstance is as the small dust of the balance compared with the power she wields as the founder of Christian homes and the director of Christian education.

It is the first, as it is the grandest instinct of the new-born soul of the parent to seek the welfare of the child. The salvation of the family and the consecration of the principle of heredity are indeed, as proved by Christian history, as potent factors in the spread of Christian civilization, as the conversion of individual souls. They are, in the Christian temple of life, the lamp whose flame is never allowed to die out. They are, in Christian society, not sporadic changeable influences for good, but the great elemental moral forces, slow, perhaps, but resistless as a glacier—primal also and magnificent.

We thus see that Christianity introduces us to experiences of life which reach back of individual opinions, and local customs, and the more personal and accidental features of life, and touches natural and primal springs in the human soul.

CREATOR OF MATERIAL WEALTH. 39

Christianity, from this point of view, is not merely personal belief nor a conventional rite, nor in any sense a something superadded to human nature. It is an appeal to, and a reinforcement of human nature. It is an inspirer of natural faculties, and can play its part most truly when the deep springs of the human soul are opened. It may be, just because of this truth, and as a condition of its action as a natural force working in the sphere of natural law, that Christianity also is subject to the universal laws of growth and decay which govern all things that live.

Everything organic and inorganic has its enemies. Life itself is but a cycle of growth and decay out of which in turn new elements of life are formed. The spiritual life of the soul is no exception to this law.

Christianity indeed, is itself the creator of virtues which, in their turn, produce wealth and culture and social ambition dangerous to the purity of the faith and the loftiest spiritual ideals. The fruit of faith is virtue, and virtue has a financial value.

Christianity is therefore a creator of wealth; but wealth, it is said, or at least its possession by the individual Christian, is the root of all social evil. Is then the spiritual life of the soul in-

volved in the fatal cycle of universal nature?
Must it grow but to decay?

Do the forces that regenerate the individual
work moral decay and industrial confusion? as
faith produces virtue, virtue creates wealth,
wealth fosters worldly ideals, and so the spirit
of religion is poisoned by the noxious weeds
which Christianity itself has produced.   Christian ideals of manhood result in new ambitions for family advancement.   This is but
another name for worldly conformity, and so
the power that ennobles society becomes the
power to destroy it.

How is this to be explained, not to say
remedied?   Is this then a contradiction?   Or
is Christianity an evil in its turn?   Is it merely
another of the forces of nature making music
in the spirit to-day to end at last in a wail of
despair?   Is all effort for betterment doomed,
and do our weary feet tread the cycle of
growth and decay, to end at last in degenera-
tion and perhaps death?

Instead of such disasters, we claim that
this feature of Christianity gives it a place
amid the facts of life—it is part of nature.   It
has its feet on the firm earth of reality.   It
denies no fact of nature and human life, otherwise proved by the senses and intellect of man.

Christianity is, above all things, a sane and

rational religion. If its head is crowned with the stars its feet are on the common highways of man. It does not propose to evade the difficulties that pertain to it, as a part of nature, by an appeal to its spiritual features. If, as a material force, it creates wealth and ambitions, which in their turn tempt the soul, it is ready to show in what natural ways that same wealth and ambition may also minister to the soul's high aim.

This ministry is by natural means, though it is claimed that in the process there is divine and spiritual reinforcement of the soul.

The intelligent Christian sees, therefore, in this struggle not a hopeless conflict of natural forces, but a phase of soul contest towards the purest and highest life. It is but the modern expression of this Apostolic principle: ''There is a law in my members warring against the law of the spirit.''

To-day it is being applied to the accumulation and use of wealth as never before in the history of the church of Christ. We have more light because we have more experience. We not only know better what is meant by the ''world'' and what by the ''church,'' but we know better what money can and what it cannot do.

We have nothing to gain from exaggeration

and less still from mere generalities. We must endeavor to see life under normal conditions. We must look into the Christian man's home and into his heart. We must treat him as a brother, and judge him at his best.

For the very forces under which he is acting, both in business and society, are generated and blessed by the Christian faith, and are to be better understood and more wisely controlled in the interests of a nobler social order.

IV.

SELFHOOD AND THE INTELLECTUAL PROGRESS OF SOCIETY.

We have considered the doctrine of Christian selfhood hitherto exclusively from the bearing it has upon the individual and the family. We have seen that salvation includes the development of individual qualities of mind and heart, which are the inalienable privileges of the new life. The vision of such a redeemed life has no horizon; eternity sweeps around it, and the heritage of the past clasps hands with the promise of the future in a divine ministry to its measureless progress.

We have seen that this faith holds the virtues and energies of the family; it claims an interest in and dominion over heredity and race; it regards the individual as completed only in the family. The promise is to the believer and his children. It lays hold upon the persistent sleepless forces of education and culture. It exalts to a sacred cultus the instinct of parenthood, which longs to see the child more wise, more strong, more honored

43

than the parent. Accordingly the Christian owes it to himself and the highest ends of his own selfhood to use all his powers for the advancement of his individual and family life along every avenue of moral, intellectual, and social progress.

But the case of Christian selfhood does not rest here; it is vitally related to the fate of society. We candidly acknowledge that society has imperative claims upon the individual. Our great anxiety is to discover how best those claims can be met. Will it be by impoverishing self and limiting personal possessions; by a doctrine of restriction or of enlargement? The Christian might well yield his fancied liberty and share his possessions and surrender his privileges for an end so noble as a regenerated and enriched social order. But the awful doubt that the sacrifice would be in vain, casts its shadow over his hopes.

In his eagerness to improve the social conditions of the poor, the oppressed, and the dispossessed classes, the doctrine of self-sacrifice, self-renunciation, and poverty is preached by the reformer with painful obliviousness to the facts of history.

Is it not a return to the old doctrine of asceticism, that virtue consists in denial and self-limitation. As Amiel asks, ''Does duty consist in obeying one's nature, even the best and most spiritual, or in conquering it?" This revival of an exploded heresy is for conquering nature not obeying it.

On the surface of it, there is much plausibility in this dogma of self-repression.

It looks so pious also. But the wiser second thought of modern life will show us that duty to one's self, to God, and even to society demands obedience to the new nature begotten in the Christian by the Holy Spirit. To ignore this doctrine of Christian selfhood is really fatal to any improvement of society and to the progress of civilization.

We believe the first duty of the Christian is to himself. His own spirit, his own business, his own family demand, by imperious injunctions of scripture and nature, obedience to the first law of all life, self-preservation, and self-development. His first duty is to grow in grace, in knowledge of life, in experience of heart and head. He can by no process of denial, limitation, or self-sacrifice do as much for the Kingdom of Christ as to prove, that by faith he has earned and entered on the possession of a large inheritance of selfhood. God's great possessions are rich, strong, full-orbed souls.

His greatest glory is in the development,

under the leading of His Spirit, of such souls
in all ages.   His church has always been rich,
and the world always blessed in proportion as
such souls have appeared in all times and
places.   Christ came to give us life—and that
life abundantly.   The inheritance of the Christian is unsearchable riches.   Religion is not a
state of either spiritual, mental, or material
poverty.   The God who endowed such large
natures as Abraham, Moses, Paul, Milton,
Pascal, and Gladstone intended vast personal
enrichment of the mind and spirit for all his
sons and daughters.

But a restriction or surrender of the physical
conditions of life, out of which grow for any
community culture, education, and the "ample page of knowledge rich with the spoils
of time," is as surely a denial to souls un-
born of this ample individual life as if we
were to close our colleges, libraries, and museums in obedience to the dictates of an obscur-
antist sect.   We can not afford to neglect the
meaning of richly endowed and developed personalities.

A great man is God's greatest gift to the
world.   Greatness is but another name for a
rich and varied nature; achievement is but another phase of personal development.   The
imperishable treasures of civilization are the

blossoming and fruitage of great minds and wills. There is a divine disregard of the fruits of the mediocre life. There is a divine care for the thoughts and deeds of transcendent spirits.

The names which have moulded the thoughts and actions of the race are numbered almost on the fingers of the hands. Aristotle, Bacon, Abraham, Paul, Jesus, Calvin, Angelo, Raphael, Newton, Darwin, Shakespeare, Luther, Goethe, Washington—we might easily give up all the others if we are allowed to retain these. Selfhood in its noblest sense was the first great concern with all these minds and in all these souls. Whether in the path of duty, or the creation of works of the imagination, or the leadership of nations, personal responsibility to the ideal life—the best—is the characteristic and dominant force of the great spirits who have made life worth living for us plain people.

It is not the creative force of a vague communal sympathy which writes The Iliad, or paints the Sistine Madonna, or rears the Parthenon. Shakespeare did not create his immortal characters, nor did Paul write his epistles because of a high level of the altruistic spirit, and a general prevalence of good wages in the nation. The artist, poet, and orator, are often self-centered, intent on large personal experiences; they are not, professedly, philanthropists. The masses and their interests, the social conditions are not greatly in evidence with them when intent upon their products of the imagination. But where would the priceless heritage of beauty, exalted thought, inspiration in the common round of life, exist to-day, had not these spirits apart poured forth the rich treasures of their individuality?

The modern individual is in danger of being lost, not only in commerce and trusts and corporations, but among mission boards and societies for philanthropy. Yet all the hope of the salvation of the world lies in the divine forces entrusted by God to the souls of great and good men and women. Personality is the richest and most ultimate elemental force in nature, as well as in the spiritual life. Without that "everlasting aye" of the individual spirit,—the experience of God in the soul we call conversion,—where were the hope to-day of any betterment of human society? Is there any betterment possible that cannot at last be traced to, and analysed into, an individual experience?

What was Paul, with that mighty evangelistic energy which flowed out of his life, but a great and overmastering individuality worked upon by the new Spirit of Christ. "I can do all things." "I am crucified with Christ." "I live; yet not I, but Christ liveth in me." Never were such sublime egoisms in all history. This man was first rich, strong, masterful in possession, and had command of all the resources of the mind and spirit, before he could pour out his treasures at the feet of his Master for the regeneration of his fellows.

Every one possessing the spirit of those great workers, saints, and confessors of the church, feels this divine impulse for personal growth and development of powers, that he may have something to give to his Savior. It is an instinct; it is an impulse to all high action and heroism of mastery over personal sloth and ignorance. Who can dictate to the soul who first learns Christ what shall be the measure of its development? Who shall say whether this Giotto of the Christian life shall continue to tend sheep upon the mountain side, or go to drink the learning of the ages at the feet of the great masters?

But education means wealth, therefore to limit wealth means to limit culture. Who will measure the disaster to Christian truth and work, if the bright spirits of those obscure youths, from Luther, the miner's son, to

Neesima, the Japanese outcast, had been denied the fruits of wealth in the great universities of their time?

I cannot limit for myself, much less for my
child, the financial requirements of my age and
profession. Twenty-five years ago a youth
might fully equip himself for professional service on half of what the post-graduate and
European course of higher instruction demand
to-day. It may be the best service I can render to the cause of the kingdom to equip fully
and train at vast cost of time and money such
a personality.

In the early days of our religious experience
we feel the fire of a great love and we dis-
count the acquisitions of the mind. We are
ready to deny and limit and restrain ourselves.
At such an hour the " self-denying ordinance "
of a peculiar community might appear to be no
loss. But as the years go by, and forces
which make for human enlightenment and the
betterment of society become better known,
we realize that no power goes so deep or lasts
so long as a great and richly endowed personality.

This is the age of authority. Not merely a
truth in the abstract, but the personality of
him who says it. A word from Frances E.
Willard, Lord Kelvin, Clara Barton, or W. E.

Gladstone on their various subjects is listened to by a whole world. If any great task is to be undertaken it can be successfully carried out only by some strong personality. This is the principle always recognized in sending ambassadors; now all service of state or church recognizes the same fact.

Both the Christian church and civic state need to-day, as never before in this realm of social activity, the service of great, strong, richly-endowed personalities. But the voluntary limitation of wealth recognizes the very opposite principle. Logically it means that suppression of natural gifts, not the development of those gifts, is the duty of the Christian man. It is laying violent hands upon powers not our own: for ye are not your own, "ye are bought with a price."

Who can measure the extent and quality of natural gifts in any youth till tested by education? But no system of training, either in home or in university, could be built upon a basis of doing as little as possible for one's self. It would prove but a "Procrustes bed" for the long-limbed genius as least, and a very fiery oven for burning up the aspirations of all the exceptionally gifted natures. The gifted souls, who regard material conditions but as accidents of life, the regal choice and buoyant ones, would see this brazen dome over their heads instead of the sky. They would be forced to live in a community where a narrow horizon was regarded as better than the wide open vault of heaven, and where more reliance was placed on artificial restraints than upon the free ordering of a redeemed and consecrated life.

V.

SELFHOOD THE AGENT OF SOCIAL BETTERMENT.

"The destruction of the poor is his poverty." These words of the inspired wise man graphically describe the sad condition of the submerged classes. The real trouble with the great mass which we want to help is their material, intellectual, and moral poverty. They are as a class weak, ignorant, defective, unfortunate, and disinherited.

No single word can fully describe the hard, cruel lot of the socially degraded inhabitants of a London or a New York or a Chicago. From the respectable and skillful laborer, who complains that his opportunities are unequal, his work uncertain, and his wages inadequate, to the defective and diseased and incapable sufferers from social injustice and industrial evils, there are all classes and conditions of people who need help and justice in the re-arrangement of the social order. All who have fallen, whether by their own vices or misfortunes, or by the injustice of others, are equally

53

in need. All who are born defective and improperly equipped for the battle of life; and all who have gone down beneath the fierce blows of an inhuman contest for their daily bread go to make up the melancholy company.

We ought not, in justice to ourselves, to allow the anarchistic rant of professional agitators, nor the crude economic heresies of some labor leaders, to prejudice us in considering the needs of the socially unfortunate and industrially oppressed. They exist, and whatever folly has been spoken in their cause they must be helped, for they threaten the very existence of our civilization.

We may admit that no single institution, or set of forces, no particular laws may be to blame for the present deplorable condition of a large part of society. But surely this condition itself is a fact of vital importance to all who love Christ and honor His church, and are loyal to the noble heritage of liberty and right received from the fathers. In the midst of the most splendid achievements of modern science and industry, thousands of thousands of our fellow-countrymen have no personal share in the fruits of this harvest. In this age of invention thousands of thousands, and many of these weak women

and helpless children, are the slaves of a hopeless industrial bondage.

> But the young, young children, O my brothers,
> They are weeping bitterly,
> In the playtime of the others,
> In the country of the free.

When the most brilliant pageant of modern
history passed through the streets of a great
European capital; when the rank and intellect
and wealth and culture of one of the mightiest
nations on earth, celebrated the jubilee of the
most magnificent reign the world has ever seen,
it was yet needful to spread a pauper's table,
and feed with the bread of charity countless
thousands of the citizens of that same rich
nation. Thus all that these submerged classes
had of the fruits of this splendid era of liberty,
wealth, and art, was a dole of charity. ''Blessed
is he that considereth the poor''; and the
blessing of God certainly rests upon the sweet
womanly heart who, amid the luxury and
splendor of the hour, considered London's
poor.

But the social wounds of the day cannot
be healed by charity, nor can the deep dis-
content, and real and fancied wrongs of the
oppressed and weak and outcast classes be
righted by private kindness and munificence.
We must approach these men and women as

brothers and sisters of a common lot. We must look into their case as fellow-citizens of a common country and partakers of a common hope.

One fact stands out conspicuously in the lurid landscape of social degradation. It is their common poverty. From circumference to centre of this world of woe, they all want something. It is all poverty—poverty of faith, of will, of resource, of physical qualities, of intellectual qualities, of moral qualities. Money is the smallest part of their needs. This want represents the general trouble, but their real wants lie deeper. What do they possess? Misfortune, injustice, sickness, and all but endless toil. They are the great disinherited.

If you would lay your hand to the work of help, you will find readily the truth of this statement. Go among them to help in the task of their betterment and you must be the possessor of something. You must be a scholar, or a physician, or a lawyer, or a nurse, or a teacher, or a capitalist, or an artist, or at least a gentleman. They do not need your poverty or ignorance or incapacity: they have more than they need of that. In whatever department of human activity you would render assistance you must yourself be a rich and strong personality; you, yourself, must be a possessor of something before you can help enrich them.

The vaunted doctrine of restriction and surrender of self-denial and poverty would be a disaster here. What these people need are educated, rich, strong, self-controlled, and cultured Christian men and women. In a word they need capital, the fruits of accumulated wealth. The qualities and possessions which the short-sighted critic of the present order objects to in the Christian are the only remedies with which social want and sorrow can be cured.

Although it has been asserted, with considerable appearance of truth, that the Christians of to-day are rich, privileged, and educated out of all sympathy with the sorrows and wrongs of the poor and oppressed, it certainly cannot be said with any degree of truth that the haunts of poverty, vice, and destitution are colonies of Christians. The Christian seems to possess a magic power of social elevation. You cannot keep him down. He is master of social forces. He solves for himself the social problem. Is it not a wonder that the social reformer has not enquired into the secret of this social buoyancy? Is it not because of this doctrine of a strong, rich, selfhood? If this doctrine is denied, or injured by any false teaching concerning the right of personal property, or education and enlargement of the individual life, will not the very conditions of a regenerated society, material betterment, and the progress of civilization be destroyed?

Now within the family of the socially degraded there is often found marked incapacity, congenital weakness, absence of will-power, and entire want of education for the real business of life. Heredity which should be an accession of physical energy, skill, and moral resource, is too often a deadly curse of disease and mental infirmity. But in a Christian home these characteristics are all reversed. Here Christianity has raised for herself a fort in the presence of the destructive forces of life, and armed and equipped every life for stern battle. On the material side of life we find industry, thrift, enterprise, and character. The farm yields plenty, the loom sings the song of abundance, the forge sends forth the fire of hope, and commerce spreads her white wings over the sea at the bidding of forces born and fostered in those active educated Christian intellects.

The wealth-producing forces in the bosom of that Christian family are as inevitable and resistless as growth and gravitation. Even in point of comparison as wealth producers, children so endowed and reared beat the world on its own chosen ground. Their faith and love have actually gone into the bone and tissue of their bodies. They have clear heads, steady nerves, powers of endurance, and economy of living that carry them far ahead of all competitors, weighted as these often are by hereditary taints, loose living, and extravagant expenditure.

But when we add to these qualities, the ideals of life, the moral and spiritual discipline which they have been subjected to, we then can form some idea of the ceaseless upward pressure into the regions of literature, art, music, and fine manners, which is continually acting on those communities, which are influenced by the forces of Christianity. Their own virtues will not let them stand still.

As the fruit of this industry and enterprise is reaped by the family, the scale of expenditure inevitably increases. In dress, in furniture, in service, and finally in residence and equipage, the gradual rise of the family fortune is manifested. Now all those virtues, all those qualities of brain and heart, are precisely what is needed for the redemption of society.

Nothing so characterized the condition of

East London when the social workers first went to carry the promise of a better life to it, as the entire absence of beauty and pleasure. In the vast aggregation of nearly two million souls there was no picture gallery, no library, no elevating amusements, no sweetness, no song, all was a dreary mud flat of stale life and endless grinding toil.

Contrasted with this gloom the Christian man, in the course of an industrious and successful life, fills his house with the treasures of art and literature and makes it sweet with music and song. Thus he gives society the surest promise of a power to rescue their depraved and squalid existence from the wretchedness of an unbeautiful life. He adorns his rooms with the choice creations of the painter and sculptor, and articles of virtu fill the nooks and corners, giving evidence of taste and travel and delighting the eye on every hand.

His children also are taught by the best masters and hear the best interpretations of music and dramatic art. They procure and read the newest literature, fitted as they are for its appreciation by their previous studies in school and college. In all probability their own pastor is the finest interpreter and keenest critic of those works of the imagination, the knowledge of which marks one as a person of taste and education. It will never occur to such a man and such a family that their actions in these particulars are other than highly proper and the inevitable destiny of the mind and spirit under favorable conditions.

It is significant that the strong religious community of New England, after performing its own proper work as makers of society and governors of the same, blossomed out as men of letters and poets. Still more remarkable to the Christian is the fact that the sacred books of his religion are acknowledged, even by men of the world, to lie at the basis of the literary culture of every modern nation. But only with such an educated taste and disciplined mind can he perceive the place of interest and power which these occupy among the immortal products of literary genius

Amid the many forces which have compelled the attention of thoughtful men to the claims of Christianity, none have been so strong as the example of a refined, educated Christian family, whose chief pleasures lie in the artistic or literary taste of its members, and whose home life was broadened and sweetened by the exercise of those rare gifts of the imagination. Luther himself was a musician, and claimed that music and song of right be-

longed to God. "Why should the devil have
all the best music?" Many a Christian man
has asked the same question again and again,
and applied it to all art and literature.

Certainly not every Christian man who suc-
ceeds in life, fills his home with the treasures
of art, and fits his family for the appreciation of literature and music, does these things
with the purpose of service. But much of
the service which Christianity renders to the
world through the actions of Christian men is
unconscious service. "They builded better
than they knew," is true of individuals and families, as it is true of communities and epochs.

It is enough to say that the person so acting
feels in some manner the call to be an example in all things. To furnish his children with
rational interests, to provide them with
healthy and sweet amusements, and to link
them by all the choicest fascinations of life to
home he knows, by instinct, is right; and it is
perhaps a recommendation to his virtue that he
has unwittingly furnished a genuine example
of what Christian forces would do for every
class of society if unhindered in their operation.

At all events, whenever the social worker
goes into the dreary regions of the poor, he
soon finds that those arts, sciences, and graces

of culture which Christian enterprise and thrift have done so much to create and accumulate, are urgently needed to sweeten and beautify the harsh and squalid places in the life of the poor. The strong, noble life of Christianity is just what the weak, degraded portion of society needs to-day. Selfhood, with all its rich, personal possessions, all its sweet graces of character and spirit, all its accumulated culture, all its hereditary skill, and moral strength, all its gathered treasures of art and literature and music, all its wisdom of family training and education,—such a selfhood is the only ground of hope for the social and industrial, as well as moral betterment of the submerged masses of society.

VI.

THE MINISTRY OF WEALTH IN EDUCATION AND PHILANTHROPY.

The greatest service that Christianity can render to-day in the cause of social regeneration, lies in the gifts which men of great wealth can render to public institutions of education, art, science, and literature, including schools of technology, and public parks, recreation grounds, and centres of comfort.

Without doubt, our greatest danger lies in the curse of a materialism, which makes a god of "barren well-being," "the idolatry of the flesh and of the ' I,' of the temporal, and of Mammon." What so certain a corrective of this tendency as the inculcation in the minds of our sons and daughters of reverence for the works of the spirit and the imagination, the divine forces in nature, and the stately march of mind in history?

Our American life needs more than the development of its material powers in mines and lumber and products of the soil and the loom: it needs a native science, a native art, and a native literature. If patriotism lies close to true religion, we must hasten to produce our own treasures of the mind and spirit before our love of country has the deathless charm, the holy fascination, which clings to classic lands of story and song.

Before even the sacred feet of Jesus consecrated the "Holy Land" it was consecrated to heroism by Joshua, Elijah, and the Maccabees. Homer and Miltiades made Greece grand; the martyrs and confessors made Rome holy. Our pilgrims to-day visit the shrines where prophets of the new era of freedom suffered and saw visions, spots made classic and dear to the heart by poets, temples filled with the products of the genius and toil of painter and sculptor, and no class of the people feels more fully the soul satisfaction of these treasures of fame than the Christian public. All aims of life, all expenditures of money, all patronage of art, and the schools which will foster and produce these things, are consistent with the best in Christianity.

These works can not be forced; they are the outgrowth of a rich soil, they require time, many of the best of them are produced in poverty and privation. Still, in every country where they have come to maturity, previous years of toil and accumulation of wealth have elapsed; education in literature, science, and art, has flourished; freedom has made some progress; men of leisure have worked themselves, or men of wealth have endowed others with the conditions of working without care. The imperious cravings of the body have first been satisfied, and the intellect and spirit untrammeled have ministered to life in those unperishable interests which ennoble humanity.

In the creation and endowment of institutions of this order, the present century has witnessed an exhibition of Christian beneficence beyond parallel in the history of the world.* We must gather up into a shining galaxy the names of the nobles and merchant princes of Venice, Florence, Amsterdam, Paris, London, and Edinburgh, like Lorenzo the magnificent, Wolsey, Richelieu, Nassau, Heriot, and a thousand others, builders of cathedrals, patrons of art, founders of universities and libraries, museums and hospitals, before we can match the opulent benefactions of the pre-

*The report of gifts and bequests for public purposes in the United States in sums of $5,000 or more during 1896, as compiled by Appleton's Annual Cyclopedia, exceeds $17,000,000. This includes large gifts made up by the combination of smaller ones, but not the ordinary denominational contributions for educational and benevolent purposes nor state and municipal appropriations to public institutions. It may be called the voluntary tax of the well-to-do toward the endowment of education and charity. In 1895 the total amount recorded, was $32,000,000.

sent era to education, missions, science, art, city adornment, and the alleviation of distress.

These gifts are counted in one city of the West alone as running into many millions of dollars. There are several new and striking features in this modern princely expenditure. Less of it is given for the building of great churches or the private glory of the benefactor in tombs and memorial structures; more of it is in the immediate direction of civic enrichment and for the advancement and enjoyment of the people. Public parks and museums and art galleries and libraries form a not inconsiderable part of these gifts. But it is in the way of great schools of the higher education—the academy, the college, and the university—that the most remarkable of these benefactions are exhibited. Characteristic of the age have been the princely endowments of great institutions of technology for the express purpose of connecting the finest results of modern scientific research and polite learning with the daily life and practical needs of the working classes. The old classic curriculum, still the backbone of all the higher learning, has been nobly sustained—indeed, in the older foundations of the East, and in the newer of the West it has secured new life and favor under this revival of generosity. But the people, as

represented in the art gallery, museum, public
park, institutions of technology, and social settlements, have been the chief benefactors.

Who have given this wealth? The mass of
this modern munificence has been Christian in
the strict sense of that term. In the case of
considerable gifts like museums and parks, the
object has been purely of a civic and educational sort; but in the case of the great majority of libraries, hospitals, institutes of technology, academies, colleges, and universities, and
social work, the givers are Christians, and their
benefactions expressly made in the name of
Christianity and for Christian service through
these channels.

We have not mentioned here the ordinary
currents of Christian beneficence, such as missionary work at home and abroad, endowment of theological seminaries and charitable
work strictly so-called; but he has a very
superficial knowledge of the Christian life who
fails to remember that a very large share of
Christian means is to-day being expended on
these and kindred claims of the church.

It is true that a very large part of this
money to-day, as in the past, has been contri-
buted by the poor. "The widow's mite,"
the poor man "out of his poverty," have con-
tributed a large part to the consecrated reve-

nues which have carried forward the work of
Christ in all ages. But it would be folly to
deny that many of our church buildings, much
of our missionary, and especially our educational, work, would be impossible without the
large benefactions of people of means.

On the other hand, it is evident that those
great foundations which give a home to Art,
Literature, Science, and Education, making original investigation possible, endowing
professional instruction, and dealing in a successful way with the problems of our great
cities, have been in the past, and are now,
the creation of large wealth. Some Christians
of to-day have recognized this fact so distinctly
that they have dedicated great fortunes to
special causes like colleges and academies in
the West, and give on principle to institutions
which are certain to endure through many generations.

Should the grateful student desire to pay
for his university education at its full money
value it would require a small fortune to satisfy the debt. All states and nations recognize this fact, and have obtained endowments either from the wealth of princes or
the taxes of a province. The fee is no pay-
ment, only an acknowledgment of gratitude,
on the part of the recipient, of the accumu-

lated wealth and learning of the people of past ages.

In all this great and wide field of service the Christian finds his grandest opportunity for the use of the means which great success has placed at his command. Many of the most conscientious give on an ascending scale and on principle, as an evidence of gratitude to God for material prosperity. This is not only an evidence of common sense, but a clear following of the apostle's precept to "lay by as the Lord has prospered us."

The great army of Christian people whom the Lord has so prospered, in all ages, would be much puzzled at many of the new doctrines concerning money, which are abroad to-day. From the days of Joseph of Aramathea to our own, the Gurneys, the Buxtons, the Baxters, the Coats, the Spicers of Great Britain, and the Hardies, the Slaters, the Dodges, and the Swetts of America, have looked upon their wealth as consecrated, in large measure, to this special form of service.

And they, with such noble princes, as John of Gaunt, David of Scotland, the leaders of the Commonwealth of England, and the Covenant of Scotland, with Lady Huntington, Lord Overton, and many more, would be much astonished to learn that the service which reflected glory on their age and untold benefit upon generations following, was no true Christian service at all. If then, the Christian man of to-day is to follow in such godly and noble footsteps, he must attend to business and regard his financial success as prosperity from the Lord.

We may be prejudiced in this matter by much of the glaring inconsistency of Christian men in their modern business methods. We may be confused by the conspicuous eagerness of all classes of Christian people for material prosperity. We may be amazed by the fact that many Christians who are so prospered of the Lord neither "lay by" nor give under impulse; but we are to remember that we live in a country and an age when material interests are the engrossing concern, and when even our Christian teachers are sorely tempted to make material comfort the only test of success in life.

Thus arise on the one hand, within the church, critics of the social order who deny to Christians the right to the accumulation of such wealth at all or to the cherishing of such ambitions. The Psalmist's description of the man that feareth the Lord goes for nothing with them. It looks like a promise from another religion: " His seed shall be mighty upon earth. . . . Wealth and riches shall be in his house.'' If they had lived in the days of Ruth, they would have been ashamed of Boaz because he was a man of wealth. Wealth, worth, and valor, or any conspicuous trait or possession that gives individuality, power, distinction, and constitutes a man sheik, chief, patron, or benefactor, is in the estimation of this class of thinkers a mark of vanity and inconsistent with the spirit of Christ. These regard the subject from the religious viewing-point.

On the other hand, there are those who on economic grounds consider the possession of great wealth by one person as in itself an evidence of the robbery of some other. Crude as this theory of wealth is, it becomes a powerful argument in the hands of a man of the world exposing the inconsistencies of Christians.

Christians have, by their own profession, renounced the world; what right have they to the possession of wealth and worldly distinction? Thus they argue. This tone gets into conversation, this criticism becomes the vogue, and it seems at first sight pious to agree with it. But amid all this pretension to a superior piety on the one hand, or to a one-sided political economy on the other, we may safely take our position on the ground of the historic examples of the men of wealth and distinction, who have been the protectors of the poor, the patrons of art and science, the founders of schools, and the promoters of missions in every age of the church's history.

VII.

CHRISTIAN SELFHOOD DISTINGUISHED FROM WORLDLY CONFORMITY.

In considering the operation of Christian virtues, both in the individual heart and the family life and through society, in the former chapters, we have dealt with actions and ideals which may reasonably be regarded as the normal Christian course of life.

We have not considered gross acts of worldliness, nor ideals that every one regards as apostacy from the spirit and purpose of Christ. We have done so to avoid exceptions, monstrosities, and all peculiarities of locality, age, and personal idiosyncracy. We have been interested in the "specimen of general value."

Some may think we have allowed too much of the spirit and ways of the world to belong to Christian society, and so begged the whole question, or at least acknowledged that historical Christianity had failed to stem the tide of worldly conformity. The latter part of this criticism, we indeed allow, has considerable force. This is the whole ground and reason of the present writing. We have sought, in leading up to this position, however, to show that this conformity is not the result of special acts of sin done apart from the normal life, or particular forms of pleasure, amusements, occupations, or avocations, in themselves inconsistent. Nor does it lie in exalted rank, genius, or great wealth.

A paradox seems to face us here; for every observer of the progress of society sees in the Christian community which accumulates wealth, and rises to distinction in arts, letters, and civics, a gradual conformity to ideals of life and practices in personal and social conduct that must be classed as worldly.

This is a social disaster. The patriot who hailed in the robust manliness of the first Christian's faith, the promise of a new social order is disappointed; and the Christian thinker who saw in that same shining devotion of the soul to Christ the power of a new type of manhood is sad at heart, the prophet of God who thought he saw the first rays of the new heaven and the new earth dawning turns away and weeps. No disaster is so terrible to a sympathetic heart as the loss of hope concerning an expected salvation of the people: "We hoped that it was he which should redeem Israel."

The modern thinker and lover of men, who

has seen system after system of truth tried, and expedient after expedient of reform fail, sees the gradual dominance of the worldly spirit over Christianity with keen disappointment, for it began so favorably and promised so much.   But experience has taught him to be more cautious than former thinkers, in his opinions as to the real source of the evil and the remedy that will cure it.

Could we say that it is wrong for a Christian man to desire personal excellence, either in intelligence or character, wrong for him to seek the education of his family in all graces and refinements of manner, as well as in the schools, and the studios; wrong for him to possess property; wrong to order his household affairs beyond the bare sustenance of the body,—then we could provide a cure, and one not impossible of adoption. For such ideas have prevailed in many instances in the past; and sumptuary and socialistic schemes have given temporary satisfaction and hope to many earnest souls.

It would thus be quite possible for us to meet the emergency by obedience to a prescribed form of dress, the practice and avoidance of certain amusements and recreations, and the adoption of particular rules regarding the use and ownership of wealth. But we have seen that conformity does not consist in external actions; that it cannot be overcome by a new rule, but by a new spirit. We have seen that it grows in soil prepared by Christian virtue; that it is a persistent, natural, and eternal tendency in human nature; and must therefore be met by forces as persistent, natural, and eternal, acting on that same nature.

Conformity is the crossing of the invisible line which separates the Christian virtue of self-improvement from the vice of self-seeking. It turns the evidences of God's favor into opportunities of self-indulgence and pride. It is a spirit, a tendency, a change of emphasis, an ideal of life produced by gradual, subtle, invisible changes in the attitude of our spirit towards the world in manners, condition, and opportunities of the whole life. It is another instance of the universal law of all things that live to lose their pristine purity,—"to vaunt in their youthful sap at height decrease and wear their brave state out of memory."

We have forgotten that this law applies to the soul; that it moves with a resistless elemental force over the life of nations, and that it can be met, if at all, only by laws of equal persistence and range. It is another illustration of the great spiritual truth that "the eternal life must be eternally reconquered."

History severely teaches us that all artificial remedies for this great evil in the human heart and society are worse than vain.
They invite reaction, they end in disaster, and
spread a deeper and more lasting moral ruin
around us.   Such attempts have brought contempt upon the strenuous souls who have seen
more in life than personal pleasure.   They
have set back the hands of the clock of Christian progress, and given nature an opportunity
to revenge herself on us for our folly.

In our age the relation of natural forces to
virtue and social life is better known and more
considered by Christian people—Nature—with
the capital letter indeed—is baptized into the
Christian church.   We are therefore in a position to estimate the natural forces that from
generation to generation act upon Christian
people, as they act upon all others.

We remember that the very purpose of
grace is to change, correct, improve, or regenerate nature.   But it is now recognized that
such operations are slow, subject still to law,
and will revert to old crudities and degenera-
tions the moment the improving impulse is
removed.   Nay, the encouraging fact is discovered that Nature wants to improve rather
than otherwise.   All her myriad seeds are
seeking favorable soil, and ready to take ad-

vantage of every friendly push or suggestion
that comes along. We know indeed that
every improvement in flower and animal, in
mind and morals, has come about in just this
way. The overwhelming power of little
things has been forced upon us at the point
of the bayonet of science. What worms have
done to plow and fertilize the soil of the whole
earth, the elemental changes produced by
forces all but invisible and creatures apparently insignificant, are the commonplaces of
modern science.

The analogies of nature teach us that regenerative and purifying energies in the moral
world must act largely on the same principles. And most certainly all those forces of
Christianity which act principally on generations of people through long periods of history, come under the operation of the same
general laws as lie at the basis of continued
improvement in nature. Under this light the
conversion of the individual soul is the first
conscious impulse towards the higher life,
both for the individual and society; but it is
not an unrelated event apart from the spiritual series which has been going on in Christian
society from the beginning.

And its reality is evidenced by the propaga-
tion of a new life to others. Such a force will

take advantage of every aid or suggestion of betterment for its individual and social improvement. It is entirely beyond our province to discuss the theology of this doctrine,—as to whether this impulse is supernatural and a communication of divine energy. Our object is simply to show that being here, as the unique and magnificent contribution of Christianity to the regeneration of the moral life of the world, its final fruits and crowning triumphs over society, come by the operation of natural law in the sphere of nature.

Its operations are not helped, but frustrated, by any and all expedients which rule it out of nature, which make it exceptional, local, accidental, and subject to arbitrary laws of life.

Christianity is thus a part of Nature in the broadest sense of that term. It is the crown and glory of those inspiring mental and spiritual forces which save men. It comes upon our life with imperial commands, with gracious and resistless persuasions. It leaves no part untouched and suffers no rival claimant to power.

If, then, it is to continue to operate on society as it operates on the individual soul, and if it is to act with the full force of this elemental moral energy on the man of education and wealth to-day, as it acted on the first Christians, we must find some explanation of the Christian life which recognizes and gives full force to this universal principle in our religion. We must find an ideal of society which puts in its right place this primary instinct of the Christian to self-improvement; which makes him a powerful factor in the production of wealth; which gives him social buoyancy and forces him into eminence; which bestows such qualities of mind and heart as make him a moulder and leader in the best society; which creates even the noblest forms of art and literature, and impels him to lay the foundations of strong, free, great nations and, in a word, confers on him this victorious element of life which conquers the world on it own battle-ground.

VIII.

PERSONAL SERVICE THE NEW IDEAL OF CHRISTIANITY.

It is easy to criticise, and break down: it is difficult to build up and create. We have no inclination, as the habit of some is (following the example of Carlyle), "to rave at everything and propose nothing."

We must find a principle of life in relation to the wealth of the Christian which shall recognize all the facts of nature and religion enumerated and illustrated in these pages. It must first of all recognize the inviolability of personal liberty and the personal ownership of property. It must, on the other hand, be able to deal with this persistent and unsleeping tendency of human nature to deteriorate and lose the pristine simplicity and love and zeal of the highest. It must be an honest effort to cure a real trouble in the social life of Christian peoples, more dangerous in proportion as they are more prosperous, old, and settled. It must not cripple the Christian's energies nor handicap his functions as a wealth

82

producer. It must not build an artificial Chinese wall about his life, nor make his manner of life peculiar, local, or unnatural. It must not interfere with his political or civil liberty, nor with his duty to himself in the development of every power of the body or the mind in the large outlook of modern Christian culture or service. And it may be added that it ought not tend to create a special sect or church out of the people who adopt it as an ideal of life.

We want in fact, a *novus ordo secularum,* but not in the spirit of Separatists from the old order, in the material and political sphere of our life. The new order of the ages may be found to be nothing very new after all: indeed, to us, it comes with all the more assurance of value as something which has been tried, on a limited field at least, and proved so far, successful.

Experienced and practical minds have a decided distrust of social and religious panaceas which are announced as absolutely sure cures, hitherto unheard-of truths. Truths which the Christian church has for two millenniums entirely overlooked, and are only now discovered by the new social prophets, are on that ground alone to be received with distrust and applied with great caution.

The remedy proposed in these pages has no such peculiar claims to our attention. It is not a mystery hidden in the ages, but a principle of life and action which all truly spiritual souls have recognized and acted upon.

It is the use of wealth, not its limitation, which alone can furnish such a principle and ideal for the new order of the ages. This principle has been recognized and acted upon by all those individuals and families whose life work and character have already been referred to as examples of the wise and virtuous stewards of wealth. In every case where Christian families are to-day exercising large influence for good order, honor, purity, benevolence, and philanthropy, this has been the principle of their family life. It is simply because these families have been so few and exceptional to the great mass of our Christian people that this principle has not been felt, as it should have been, on a national or universal scale.

We believe the time has fully come for its universal acknowledgment and adoption by advanced Christian thinkers and workers, as the fundamental principle in their social life. To this end, it must be fully set forth in all its wide scope and deep reach, through every form of modern thought and activity.

What hope have we, that a theory of life, long known but not universally adopted, will become a new force to-day? What reason have we for believing that the Christian church will fall in love with this ideal now, if she has not done so before? There are several reasons, in the trend of modern Christian thought and the change of emphasis on ideals of social obligation, which warrant the belief that we are entering upon a new era of Christian character and service. There is a growing conviction in the breasts of earnest Christian men that, through the long years of heroism and self-sacrifice in the history of European and American Christianity, we have won only the outward framework of liberty. We have secured only the political form. The essential spirit of liberty in the mastery of our own evil tendencies we have not yet won.

The very successes of the church have, as time passed by, confounded her with the forces of the world. And consequently new ideals of life must be adopted to infuse new spirit and purpose into her thought and action in the future.

This is a return to first principles, but the human mind, in returning to first principles either in art, politics, or religion, never goes back with the same mental or moral equipment with which the first disciples adopted those principles. This, in reality, is our ground of hope. We do not to-day advise a return to first principles and to the simplicity of the Gospel, ignorant of those truths concerning human nature, history, and economics which characterized the first disciples. They had the future, like a trackless forest, all before them. We have returned upon their footsteps to find this forest a cultivated country, full of cities and busy with mills and mines, and all the wonders of art and literature. We have, above all, the incomparable object-lessons of two thousand years of the operation of Christian ideas upon the spiritual, artistic, political, and social forces of human nature.

We do not possess, it is true, the fiery zeal and the splendid enthusiasm of those first disciples, who, under the expectation of an immediate return of the Lord Jesus and a final consummation of all things, were looking and working for a new heaven and a new earth. Our hearts are sobered by, and our minds opened to, the larger and more mysterious facts of life, which, under the long discipline of the Holy Spirit for nigh two thousand years, have been impressed upon us.

We have seen that it is apparently God's purpose that even the Kingdom of Christ shall come under the dominion of those laws of the universal life which require ages and millenniums for their complete fulfillment. We have discerned the reach and power of heredity and the force of example and custom handed down from generation to generation. We do not readily to-day build false hopes of a speedy success even in good works. We rely very largely on education, or processes of development and betterment, that go on from one generation of the godly to another.

To return therefore, to the first principles of our faith, does not mean retrogression. It is not the action of the sectarian visionary dazzled with the brightness of the past but blinded to the lessons of the present. It is the action of the scholar and believer, who knows and loves the great ideals of the past, but who brings to that past also the treasures of experience and discipline of the present. This is the condition of all true human progress, civil and religious.

We are in a state of mind to-day when no lesson in church or state is being lost upon us. We are impatient of idiosyncracies, of half-truths, of paths that lead nowhere, of grinding cycles of meaningless misery to society. We love realities. We prefer to be doing something rather than dreaming about doing it. If we have not the lofty visions, the purifying spiritual enthusiasm of the early days, we have the caution and practicality come of long experience; and we share equally with them the ultimate conviction that life is vain if we cannot redeem men from the power of sin, and lift society into a loftier plane of living, both in its material and moral experiences.

However much thinking men may differ as to methods in the accomplishment of the great work of the Kingdom, both as regards the evangelization of the unbelieving world or the Christian culture of the professors of faith in Christ, there is no difference in the facts of history brought up to date. We know what truths have been emphasized, and what ideals of life have been set before men during those years of Christian instruction in the past; and we know just what the results are.

No one regards the present situation as satisfactory. There is the most ominous agreement on this point, both by those who love the church and by those who hate her. The one part may say it is because the true doctrine of Christianity has not been accepted and acted upon by the people, and the other part may say the true doctrine has not been preached, but both agree that Europe and America, in

the nineteenth century of our Lord, does not
present that face of heavenly splendor, that
front of power, and that heart unspotted from
the world, which the Founder's character and
its first disciples' faith and heroism led us to
expect.

Another class smile cynically at this heated
discussion, believing that both these disputants
are missing the great lessons of the past and
the real requirements of the present. They
think that all altruistic plans for social betterment are doomed to failure. But because certain lines of action and systems of doctrine
have not produced upon the world all that
their first sanguine promoters expected, it by
no means follows that those doctrines were
false or those methods foolish. They may
have been better for their own age than other
ideas and methods regarded with more favor
to-day. On the other hand, doctrines and
methods that saved and inspired the lives of
men of the past may have become powerless
to accomplish the same class or extent of
results in the present.

Most certainly the failures to produce the
best results on any universal scale justify the
reconsideration of old ideas and methods in
the light of all the history and experiences of
the Church of Christ. This thought, it will

be observed, is based upon the fact that the history and experience of the church comes from the instruction and guidance of the Holy Spirit. If this position is not granted to us by all Christian thinkers, we are paralyzed in our efforts for improvement. But we believe none will deny it. It is an evidence of the continued life and power of the church to be able to adapt her methods and to better understand her doctrines in the new light which is continually breaking out of the Word of God and the book of history.

Because of this hopeful principle of Christian progress many conservative thinkers to-day are looking back to the life of the Founder of our faith for their guidance and inspiration. They are coming again to His teachings and the teaching of His apostles and first disciples with new difficulties and new questions, but at the same time with fresh enlightenment and fresh ideals growing out of the mistakes as well as the victories of the past.

Our age is one of reconstruction in church and state: new methods are demanded, new responsibilities are being felt, and new meaning and forces are being added to old doctrines. There never was a time of change when so many indications of success were present or so many reasons for hope pressed themselves upon earnest, open-eyed workers and thinkers.

During the now closing century the revolution in European politics, the appearance and growth of the Western Republic, the changes in modern life and thought produced by steam, electricity, and the mechanical inventions, the spread of popular education, and the marked increase in the material prosperity of the common people have all helped to create new ideas about and impose new duties upon wealth.

New social claims and physical wants have arisen in places long deprived and unregarded. New compunctions have awakened in the breasts of possessors. New avenues of service have been opened or at least seized for the first time. New powers of appreciation of the social and economic bearing of Christian doctrine have been developed by the teachings of the church in the minds of the general public.

The church herself is braced to a higher conception of duty and to a diviner life by the spread of her own principles. No one speaks with contempt to-day of men of another class or persuasion, and all genuine souls are eager to find a solution of the problem of life which will give play to the redeemed powers of manhood in a regenerated social order.

IX.

MODERN LESSONS ON CHRISTIANITY AND WEALTH.

It may be well to state in brief those truths the church has learned about herself in her relations to wealth and social life, and what both Christianity and the world have also discovered as to the social function and real value of material prosperity.

We practical moderns have lost somewhat of the poetry of life, but we have gained in clearness and consequent sincerity. It is a process often necessary before we can gain the true basis of a new poetry. The church is more sincere about herself to-day, she is getting back to a love of reality and simplicity, and is feeling already the breath of a divine inspiration. This comes of a new sense of the value of the character and teaching of her divine Founder. Especially has interest deepened by considering the practical bearing of His example upon our thought and action in our present earthly career.

During the first few centuries of our era

Christianity was under the sway of a one-sided doctrine of separation. The crystal purity of her conception of personal holiness, in contrast with the dark facts of the heathen life out of which she was saved, created a distinct separation in character. The new ideals of the divine Kingdom in contrast with the cruelty and oppression of the kings and conquerors of those unsettled times bred a sacred passion of hatred for tyranny disguised as governments of the world. Those forms of life and powers of government which Christianity found to be her deadly enemies she naturally thought of as doomed to certain destruction.

In her teaching she gradually separated the sacred from the secular. "Man was broken up into parts an outer and inner." "The world into earth and heaven, hell and paradise." "This was done it is true in order to construct man more profoundly and truly. But Christianity has not digested this powerful leaven. She has not yet conquered her true humanity; she is still living under the antinomy of sin and grace, of here below and there above. She has not penetrated into the whole heart of Jesus." These words from one of the profoundest spiritual thinkers of our age show just how such a nature as Amiel's, always yearning after the "totality of being," was affected by this one-sided phase of Christian teaching.

Thus for ages the mighty spiritual forces generated by the Gospel were used up by believers largely in the effort to save their own souls from the city of destruction. The world and its material interests had nothing for them; left to brood and dream if of a mystical turn of mind, to scheme and plot for a spiritual dominion over the government of this world if of an active and ambitious genius.

At last a religious life became possible only by physical separation from the world of men, and the burial of the body in the living tomb of cell or cave. This phase of exaggeration might have passed away, or been sloughed off for a more rational doctrine, if the error had touched only the lives of nuns and monks, anchorites and recluses. But it affected the thinking and action of the common people also. They were compelled by the exigencies of their labor for daily bread to reconcile a doctrine which degraded the physical nature with the imperious cravings of that same nature supposedly implanted by the Creator. They could not retire from the world, they had still to work in the open field of public life.

But among those common men also great

spiritual forces had been awakened, especially at the period of the Reformation in
Europe. They were still under the dominion
of "here and there," and "outer and inner,"
"a secular and a sacred." Individualism had
done its best for them under this scheme of life,
and perhaps also its worst. They were saved,
their life was in heaven; religiously they were a
separate people; they sought a new country.
But materially, politically, and as the founders
of families, the creators of states and nations,
they were yet living on earth. They were
bound by its laws, statute and natural, they
were influenced by material interests and by
human ambitions perhaps more than they
thought.

Gradually, insidiously, but with fatal thoroughness, their religious experience, prevented
from becoming a universal principle of human action, became a mere form and fashion of the soul, often bereft of reality, always
shorn of power. It was found impossible
to continue to attach the energies and interests of the new-born Christian soul to a
domain of life limited in time, place, and subject. Religion, largely bereft of the transcendent interest of present reality, was relegated to churches, priests, and dying people.
The courage, ambition, talent, industrial en-

ergies of men, professedly Christian, were given to government, business, science, art, and letters. Wealth production, as the common measure of all forms of activity, claimed its leading share of those powers, and Christian men manifested the qualities of their new life by activities along those lines thus opened up to them by the social conditions and religious ideas of their age. Balzac, with a certain contempt for the thrifty virtues of the Huguenots, points out that all Protestants are characterized by this same trait. They profess great unworldliness, but are the great traders and manufacturers and money-getters of the world.

Thus the intellectual and spiritual powers of man awakened by Christianity, perverted by a one-sided doctrine of life, are diverted with resistless energy into channels of money-making, which in turn destroy the original spiritual conception of life revealed by Christianity. Such facts as these writ large on the page of history teach us just exactly what the church can do in the old way; not, we must be allowed to say, with the "old Gospel," but with the old way of interpreting the Gospel, especially in its relation to our present life.

The method which resulted, in a few centuries, in the conformity of the church to the

world and the conversion of the divine regenerative energies of Christianity into engines of
personal ambition and wealth production must
necessarily be defective. Some saving truth
has been missed, some governing corrective
idea has been lost sight of. The emphasis
upon the salvation of the individual soul, upon
its eternal destiny, upon the transcendent
importance of the spiritual, has been overdone.

The mutual and corrective truth that the
secular is sacred, that "the there is here," that
"heaven is in the heart," and "the Kingdom
of God within us," must be recognized by
the church. We know that as we cannot fly
with one wing, we cannot be saved by a one-
sided Christian faith and life. The individual
is the source but not the end of power, the
seed of a divine Kingdom is in his heart, but
it must be sown in the soil of the present life
and gather its larger nature from all influences
of earth and sky. The social salvation is an
integral part of the coming of the Kingdom.
Unless the individual lives to save society he
can not live unto the larger life of the Spirit
of Christ.

Nay, society will turn her forces of evil upon
his selfish spirituality and destroy it root and
branch. Christian thinkers have learned that
a doctrine of personal salvation unrelated to

society and mundane existence is helpless to redeem the world for Christ and to keep the church unspotted from the world. They know that to awaken in the soul of man the ideals and energies which the Gospel has power to do, as far as the development and culture of the individual is concerned, and throw him upon life without the restraint of the social obligations immediately growing out of the possession of these powers, is to result finally in the deterioration and the corruption of the church. And the hopeless, sickening sense of such a cycle of victory and defeat, returning upon all Christian effort, brings despair to the hearts of the lovers of humanity. They are convinced, therefore, that these two thousand years are sufficient to have taught the universal church the necessity of a new method, comprehensive of all life, and embracing the use of every energy in the regenerated soul.

Side by side with this lesson, and throwing much light upon it, have also arisen new ideas concerning the obligations and functions of wealth. We know better to-day, Christian men, and men of the world also, just what wealth can and can not do. Paradoxical as it may seem, wealth is both exalted and abased to-day in the estimation of thoughtful men. Used to benefit others—wisely, as administered by men of great experience in affairs—it has all but unlimited powers of good; used to gratify appetites and personal luxury, it is as the apples of Sodom, dust and ashes between the teeth. Used to equip, educate, refine, enlarge by travel and broader social service, it is the handmaid of all noble spirits, the means of cultivating the peculiar grace for which princes and lords of old were counted excellent and generous. Used to aggrandize family greed, ambition, and trusts, it is an instrument of tyranny and ominous to the safety of society.

As long as the passion of wealth getting is on the man these great ideas of the age may be absent or feeble, but sooner or later the lessons of the common experience come home to him. "Is the game worth the candle?" Is all this worry, toil, and defeat of the higher end of life wise, in view of the limited power of money at best? These reflections come with redoubled force when it is rather a question of heaping up more than one can use.

The Christian man must be even more deeply impressed with these facts touching the moral value of wealth. The initial impulse of an earnest, ambitious, industrious life may have carried him far; he pauses to contrast the ideals with which he started out, with the ideals and purposes now governing his life. He may have missed the personal culture largely because he has confounded the means with the end.   He finds himself in possession, but not capable of enjoyment.   He has no time and no inclination for pleasures and ser- vices which he had hoped would be greatly possible by means of the larger wealth.   His own inability to obtain the best, and the re- quirements of less fortunate lives to share his abundance, come with combined force upon his spirit.   Or even if he has carried a finely balanced life all along, knows himself the larger, deeper life of the spirit, has kept in touch with the widening, uplifting breath of the modern intellect in science, art, and litera- ture,—such a man, in the new atmosphere of social obligations, will best read his larger op- portunities, for he knows what faith and love, education and refinement can accomplish.

We are thus facing the problem of wealth as no other period of Christian history has been able to do.   We are face to face with its powers and its limitations, its obligations and its rights, with an equipment of experience and thought which no other time possessed.   The Christians are possessors of the wealth and power, the science and the art, the education and freedom which it is proposed to use for higher ends. This puts us in a very different position from those who are discussing a subject of which they know nothing, and disposing of means which they never created.

This wealth has been made under Christian forms of government and rules of social and business life which have grown up in so-called Christian lands. In close daily touch with the industry and skill of the workman and the enterprise and genius of the manager and inventor have been the knowledge, the prayers, the hopes, and impulses of Christian lives. We can not say let us wait till we form a Christian Society before we can tell what the effect of wealth upon Christians will be. We know now. We have seen its best and its worst under the old ideals. We are not satisfied. It has not done as much for us as it promised at starting out. It has not done as much for our families and our nation as we have just reason to believe it can do. We are conscious of needs it has never ministered to and conditions from which it has not saved us nor ours. These thoughts deepen in the hearts of Christian men; they are in the air; the age is favorable, on account of them, to new ideals of the use and power of wealth. We go back, therefore, to some first principles of our Christian faith, sobered, matured, and, we believe, chastened in heart and mind; for we know that on this great experiment of a spiritual life utilizing the physical forces of wealth in the creation of a new social order rests the hopes of mankind.

X.

SIMPLICITY IN LIVING.

Under the general subject of the ''New Ideal of Life'' as manifested in the Christian use of wealth, let us proceed to illustrate the largeness and sweep of the thought.

If it controls us only at odd times, in our more reflective moments, under special impulses, wrought up feelings, and in hours of worship; but is not comprehensive, active, when we are oblivious of the motive of our action; pulsing through life like our heart's blood, it is an inadequate remedy for the evils we desire to cure.

It remains then for us to show how pervasively, how universally, how simply, and how naturally it will act throughout all our life.

One of the happiest and most helpful results of such an ideal would be in the return to greater simplicity in our manner of living. This is entirely different from the ascetic habit. Simplicity is not exclusive of elegance, but of luxury. Vulgar people spend large sums to furnish their houses in imitation of the fashionable rich, with the result described by David Lyall in the house of Ann Laidlaw, "discriminating people wondered how it was possible to gather so much that was hideous and costly in one place." As the expensive is not necessarily beautiful, the simple is not necessarily ugly.

An elegant simplicity is characteristic of good breeding, gentle manners, and old family traditions. It may, in a sort, be considered the real basis of gentility. The rich parvenu thinks otherwise, and makes up in lavish display and ostentatious luxury what he lacks in family portraits and fine old silver. But the real gentleman is known as much by the simplicity of his habits as by the castle and the crest.

This is not a mere fashion but a principle of life. Its tap root is in the very deepest soil of life. It concerns what a man eats, drinks, wears, surrounds himself with. It is in a manner the physical basis of life—the clothing of his soul. It is eminently personal and often presents to the youth the first battle-ground between the spirit and the flesh. From the standpoint of taste alone some people choose a simple and unostentatious manner of life; but if we are to insist upon it as a principle for the guidance of Christian society we must show that it is other and greater than a matter of taste.

What spiritual principle is involved? This namely, that to the Christian wealth, on its material side even, is sacred. That food, drink, raiment, furniture, are all for use, not gratification. That they have a sacred ministry, intimately related both to manners and to morals. That waste, luxury, intemperance, display, selfish excessive expenditures are as much sins in the eye of God as dishonesty and lying. This is what Jesus indicated when, at the close of the miracle of feeding the multitude, he said, "Gather up the fragments that remain that nothing be lost." The material basis of life, on this ground alone, is sacred, and we indicate in this close personal action our sense of responsibility for its use. We bring those preëminently personal and physical functions of life and social habits under the sway of a principle, not of mere self-denial but of administration.

Assuredly those personal habits lie at the basis of all morals, all gentlehood, all usefulness. I can hardly reconcile the thought of a Christian man being a gross eater. Yet I have known many such. Of Christian people, lavish, luxurious, and even intemperate, how are we to speak? It is largely because the divine grace of simplicity has not been taught; because the physical basis of spirituality has not been insisted upon. "Your bodies," says the Apostle, "are to be the temple of the Holy Ghost," they are to be washed with pure water. Revelling and riotous living were the characteristics of the heathen: simplicity and sobriety of manners were to be the marks of Christians. Nothing said here should be construed as finical or small criticism of the minor morals and refined habits of life either in food, dress, or equipage. These things may be elegant and choice, and yet be perfectly consistent with this principle of simplicity. We are not arguing for a deal table, a sanded floor, and unwashed waiters.

We have already insisted that any remedy for conformity to the world which implies interference with personal liberty in the ordering of expenditures is as vicious as it is vain. The principle of simplicity can be seen illustrated alike in the homes of the great and the humble. One feature is common to both: a certain intelligence and refinement, a way of looking at possessions as means to an end, and a sense of responsibility for the uses to which they put even the material things of the world. The adoption of the simple aphorism, that "we eat to live but do not live to eat," would save many of us from deep pitfalls that swallow up health and morals. Simplicity is not only consistent with dainty habits of life, it nourishes and cherishes them as Christian graces. These are a sweet and gracious fruit of Christian civilization and peculiarly treasured by cultured women. Refined and dainty manners at table have always been the marks of a true lady. Chaucer, in his sweet picture of the Prioresse, gives this note:

"At mete was she wel ytaughte withalle;
She lette no morsel from her lippes falle."

But what a gross inconsistency that, with such clean sweet personal habits, women should have tolerated the Sybaritic luxury, and the orgies of drinking common to fashionable society for five hundred years. We have nothing to say against flowers, crystal, silver, and spotless damask, pink teas, and dainty luncheons; nothing to say against banquets of State or club dinners; for this is not a plea for a sumptuary law. Our claim is that a simple manner of life is consistent with gentlehood and refinement, that it fosters instead of destroying them. Our contention is that excess, intemperance, luxury, display, is not only vulgar but sinful; that it is a denial of the sacredness of personal bodily functions, and an

adoption, at the very basis of individual conduct, of heathen ideas of life.

But can it be reasonably maintained that the
general habits of Christians, as far as relate to
the table, dress, furniture, social expenditures,
and amusements, are excessive, often actually
intemperate, and entirely quite too luxurious
for those making their profession? Let it be
distinctly understood here that by "their profession" is not meant a special profession of
self-denial, limitation, and renunciation of the
"good things" of this life, but simply a profession to regard the spiritual life as nobler
than the life of the flesh, and that all which
goes to make up gentleness, purity, strength
in body and soul is their sworn friend, and all
that renders them vulgar, selfish, and weak is
their sworn foe.   In this sense it can be said, in
all charity, that our present Christian society is
luxurious and excessive, and regards the possession of wealth as a means to personal gratification rather than a power to reach a higher
life.

The condition of woman, it is said, is the
measure of any civilization, her personal habits
the best test of social refinement anywhere, but
it is true also that her social ambitions are the
best indications of the prevalence or absence
of conformity to the world.   It is to satisfy

her social ambitions that many men in business and professional life, live beyond their means and scatter both fortune and life in the process. Woman is a creature of stronger moral fiber, of purer life, of greater courage in the time of sickness and disaster than man. But she is more dependent on surroundings when fortune smiles. Her social graces thrive best in the sunshine, and she expands and rises in conscious power when wealth sets her on high.

Thus the first signs of growing social ambitions appear among the female members of the family. The daughters have been sent to fashionable schools, they have had a little fortune spent upon them for music and other accomplishments. They must now have some stage worthy of their powers, natural and acquired. What is wealth if it can not win social recognition? What is education if it can not secure fashionable friends? What is business success if it does not procure a social throne? For these purposes, with the attendant expenses of house, carriage, furniture, dress, clubs, and sports, the great body of wealth in our Christian homes is lavished.

Under these ideals the thought of responsibility and sacred use of wealth, even in its bearing on their own life, is absent or unheeded. The wealth is theirs; what they require therefore to minister to their own appetites or pride or ambition appears the first and exclusive purpose of expenditure. Its use for higher ends is a side issue. They do not say "my duty is to be educated, refined, accomplished, useful, for the purpose of illustrating in my own life the beauty and nobleness of Christ; for the purpose of making my home happy and a centre of comfort and pleasure to father, mother, and friend." They do not see that qualities of heart and head, combined with education and refinement, are not only the only things worth having in themselves, but are passports and creators of all the best society.

The simplicity which characterizes the spiritual nature under this sense of obligation is the evidence of real worth and the ground of social recognition, while it breaks no fortunes and shortens no lives.

The luxury and extravagance which mark the carnal nature and selfish liver is the evidence of pretense and the precursor of social failure, while it often disrupts business and hastens death.

The thoughtful Christian husband and wife must consider the effect of an ideal like this in the early years of their domestic history. The children will become largely what they are habituated to. They are the creatures of atmosphere, habitat, and example. If they find evidences of a refined and enlightened simplicity in the home, in most cases they will honor it by imitation. The traditions of the family for such gentlehood and simplicity in conduct will become part of their heritage, and the vices of a materialistic selfish life will be repugnant to them. Even with the utmost care in education and the most consistent personal example, children will sometimes show the animal traits and the most selfish disposition. No more deadly poison can enter the blood of a child than the selfishness which leads him to regard the parents' wealth as a fortunate chance for his own indulgence or ambition. This is that evil which has its ripe fruit in the "post-obits" of fashionable young roués, and the deep dishonor of waiting for the old man's death. It is a sure sign of a corrupt society, and has been rightly regarded by observers of manners like Thackeray as the final dishonor of an abandoned life.

One other consideration affects the conduct of the more thoughtful people to-day in the manner of their living. It is the contrast presented by the abundant and luxurious tables of the wealthy, and the hunger and destitution in many homes of the poor. It is no sufficient answer to say that much of this is due to vice on the part of the poor themselves, misfortunes or economic conditions over which the rich have, as individuals, no control. Nor is it material to say that much of the expenditure of the rich in dress, table, and equipage, goes to benefit trade. The truth is, that behind economic considerations is the fact of a common humanity, and when large classes of people go hungry and naked, no man of fine feelings will banquet to surfeit, or dress like Beau Brummell. The action too strongly resembles the parable of the rich man and Lazarus.

The Christian man, especially, will recognize this as a matter of spiritual discretion. He is forced by his better nature to find a principle of action which, without involving his domestic and business life in the evils of communism or indiscriminate charity, will at least save him from the charge of a heartless disregard of the sufferings of the unfortunate. He instinctively perceives that simplicity in eating and dressing are the first marks of such sympathy, and the people will perceive that the man who can so order his life has laid hold of a principle dealing with the use of wealth which renders him a promoter of general well being.

In view of the newer political economy, it is true that a thrift and simplicity which results in hoarding, and limiting of proper expenditures for the table, clothing, and furniture, are a great disaster both to the rich and poor. But the cultured, responsible Christian man who has adopted the rule of simplicity will never commit this mistake. In his house no domestic will ever need to complain of the "long prayers and short suppers." His character can never be summed up in the pithy proverb, "greedy as godly." He will be a man to whom the simplicity of Jesus has become real and the spiritual uses of material things has been revealed—one to whom life, on its physical side even, furnishes the vantage ground of high character and great usefulness. "Plain living and high thinking" will not mean sordid ways and an excuse for avarice, but a larger, purer family and personal ideal of life, and opportunity for spiritual influence. A knowledge of the ministry of things, a mastery over the qualities of things, and a divine purpose in the use of things, are what may be hoped for from the simpler manner of life. Nearer the heart of Jesus, nearer the throbbing pulse of humanity, nearer the beauty of nature we get, the simpler we become in our manner of living.

XI.

EDUCATION AND FAMILY TRAINING.

The family (the true integer of society), the power of heredity, the influence of family traditions, and the promise of God to bless our children, should be the four-square foundation on which to build Christian society to-day.

Christians commence family life with gracious and unselfish feelings in their own hearts, which they never dream of organizing into principles of family education. And they are surprised and disappointed when the children refuse to accept the spiritual ideals of life and the unselfish service of humanity which warmed their own hearts when young. We train our children for the professions with elaborate care on lines which long experience have proved perfectly adapted for the end in view. We leave the ideal of life largely to chance.

These two thousand years of a Christian gospel have not yet yielded us a science of family training and Christian education fitted to impress our own children with the preëmi-

nent superiority of the spiritual ideal and practical method of life possessed by the Founder
of our Faith. We have not seriously thought
Christian education and family training with
such ends in view possible.

Accordingly the spiritual force which we
gain in one generation we lose in another. We
do not think it strange, even, that the child
of devout parents should "cast in his lot
with the evildoers." Mrs. Humphrey Ward,
in her latest delineation of English society,
makes the only son of a tender, spiritual,
devotée mother a rake and rebel against all
law and decency. In religion we have almost
altogether elected to fight the battle against
the world, the flesh, and the devil without the
aid of the hereditary principle and forgetting
the divine promise concerning training and
education. We have handed over these forces
to the enemy, and he has used them with cruel
thoroughness against our dearest interests.

Our openly avowed purpose in education
has been to obtain for our children a good
settlement in life. A "good settlement" has
come to mean almost exclusively a "good
financial settlement." Education has been
controlled almost entirely by this idea; training in the home, when given at all, has been
toward this object. And now we are surprised

and chagrined that our children are more materialistic than we are ourselves.

The recipients of our hero-worship, whom
we have belauded in orations, held up as examples in the pulpits, mentioned with reverence at our own tables, and praised in biog-
raphies are millionaires and boss politicians.
''Business success,'' ''getting on,'' ''making
money,'' are the characteristic phrases of our
nineteenth century civilization.

Our youth want to ''get through'' college,
they do not want to be educated. In some
cases, in our great cities, where the fever has
entered the blood with greatest virulence, sons
and daughters of wealthy Christian parents
have less regard for a university training than
the children of European peasants. Even
those who do go to college are consumed
with eagerness to get done with their studies
that they may go to money making. This is
eating our corn in the green ear—poisoning
the very fountain of the intellectual life at its
source. Even for the purpose of wealth production this is suicidal, while for the ends of
a higher civilization and a spiritual ideal of life
it is altogether fatal.

Something vital is wanting here. Evidently
the absence of correct and systematic instruction by parents concerning the use of wealth.

What is society the better for the financial success of this man if his wealth is to be made only a vantage ground for a succeeding generation of grasping, materialistic children? The first effect of easy circumstances in any home should be relief from anxiety about the world. It should mean to the children the direction of the mind and heart, without distraction, to the mental and spiritual equipment of life, so that when their call to public duty comes the state and church should get their best.

It is by the operation of this principle that the artist, scientist, and literary worker is relieved, either by private munificence or public endowment, from productive toil in the early period of his life, and trained to the exercise of his highest powers. But the youth with the materialistic conception of life renounces his advantages, "sells his birthright for a mess of pottage," and the second generation of Christians lose all their spiritual advantages from the rise in life won by their parents. Indeed, they have deteriorated; for the money of the first generation was tempered by the warm impulses and kindly faith of the parents and some restraint of a spiritual kind was placed upon its use. But in the hands of the second generation, which has rejected the spiritual ideal of its fathers, and appreciates only the base residue of their worldly success, money becomes an engine of evil, destructive of the best in the man and in society.

A clear grasp of these moral uses of wealth, as related to the training and education of children, would greatly help to solve this problem of conformity to the world in our very homes. Christian parents must be led to see that the power of money in certain most vital directions is limited. They must be taught anew the meaning of our Savior's words, "a man's life consisteth not in the abundance of the things which he possesseth."

The main purpose of wealth is to educate and equip the young people for service. If they are so educated and so trained that all the powers of mind and heart are in normal, healthy action, they are on the high road to success. Success is not a return upon the old road the parents have gone, and added wealth is not the only end for an educated Christian youth. The very possession of wealth by parents should be a divine call to the children for a different kind of service. They have thus become, as it were, hostages to God for the execution of a high treaty in the interests of a more spiritual and enlightened life and a larger service for the needy and unfortunate.

Educational life at school and college must be regarded with greater pleasure and interest by the students. It is at present regarded too often as a time of restraint and deprivation. This fever of materialism must be got out of the blood of our youth, and the calmness, repose, elevation of manner, and love of study for its own sake, which belong to the healthy blood of noble youth, be injected in its place. Children must be taught that under no normal conditions of life, if they will only look at education from the right viewing point, will they ever be so happy and so honorable as when students. They must be taught the secret of enjoying the present, *carpe diem* with a new significance.

It is not because my boy may be a great statesman or a successful merchant that I love him, nor because my daughter may marry a millionaire that I love her. I love them for themselves, not for what they may achieve or obtain in the future. I am in no hurry to see them graduate. My money, won by honest toil, is now being used for a divine purpose in their education. This is, in itself, if not an ultimate fact, yet quite ultimate enough to mark an era in life and produce enjoyment. Why should they not look at the wealth of their home in the same way?

When fitly educated, it is quite possible— in many cases very desirable—that the boy should follow his father's business or professional career. It is possible, also, that a prolonged university training may not be necessary or desirable. This does not in any way alter the ideas concerning the use of wealth which such a boy ought to be taught. An education fitted to his calling and genius is the best for him. His business may be as much a trust as the artistic gift. His professional service may be as much a consecration of his energies as if he went forth to minister in a foreign land.

But if no such lofty ideas of responsibility come to the children of wealthy homes, they are in a worse condition, as far as the spiritual objects of life are concerned, than their parents. Life with them has entered the weary, dreary, monotony of materialism. "They make money to buy land to feed hogs, to make more money to buy more land to feed more hogs, to make still more money," and so on *ad infinitum*, till existence is a burden and life is shorn of its glory.

Worldly conformity has no more constant stream feeding its bitter waters than the materialism of the children of well-to-do parents. This supply is constant, partly because of the ignorance, partly because of the folly of Christian people. When we forget our own early ideals, our faith and hope of larger service for Christ and men, in the vanity of later success, the children born into our homes can see the present selfishness and worldly manners—they can not perceive the original impulses. This is our folly. We expect them to take up into their life ideas to which we attained by sweat and blood. We forget that our success has rendered them susceptible to new influences and instruction; but we do not know how to teach and apply the new forces. This is our ignorance.

Social christianity was certainly intended to grow stronger and purer as the sons and daughters of men of faith grew up in the shelter and culture of refined and educated homes. It has failed to do so, largely because Christian parents have not found in wealth its spiritual ministry and have not made it a condition of nobler service. As princes are educated to duties of state, Christian children should be educated to the service of the people. No prince would consider it a privilege to make money, because he has all that money can bring. The children of wealthy Christian homes have all that money can bring. Would they but recognize its responsibilities, they would add the princely dignity of service also to their life.

When, therefore, they are fully prepared for the work of their life, under the direction of this new ideal they will enter it with a wide outlook, with a real knowledge of the value of money, with a spiritual purpose, and with a just regard to the claims of society upon their service as privileged and fortunate persons.

Such ideals and ambitions will increase their productive energies, not only in business, but in art, science, and literature, while it will enormously increase their fitness and willingness for all forms of philanthropic service. In a generation or two this would yield us a class of spendidly equipped, public spirited citizens, and noble, devoted workers for the church.

The results of such training will tell also upon the preëminently vital subject of personal service, which the conscience of the time is demanding of all truly earnest souls.

XII.

PERSONAL SERVICE A PRIVILEGE OF WEALTH.

The note of the new philanthropy is personal service. Rich people have, almost entirely, hitherto, done such work, by proxy. In fashionable society "Marcella" is an oddity because she went to live among the people of the East End of London, and thus learn by actual contact, and by personal friendship and fellow-suffering, the real condition and thoughts of the working-classes.

Conventional Christians whose hearts have not felt the throb of the new movement can not understand this "latest fad" on the part of their "peculiar" acquaintances and friends. It is totally unlike the ministry for the church poor, where old women and sick people were visited by the parson and the good ladies of the parish, and were given blankets and provisions. Such kindly personal service to parish neighbors and fellow-members of the church has always prevailed among charitable and generous Christians. The idea of a brotherhood of humanity which could be helped only by love and sympathy shown by the rich, cultured, and strong for the weak, poor, and ignorant has overgrown the church-wall, and is shedding its fragrance in the great field of the world.

This divine impulse to personal social service lies at the heart, and surrounds, like an atmosphere, the whole of the new effort to help men known as "the Social Settlement Movement." It came from the heart and brain of a cultured student of Oxford, Arnold Toynbee, and it has found its warmest supporters among the privileged class to which he belonged.

Since Toynbee Hall settlement was established in 1885, Miss Lathrop, of Hull House, Chicago, informs us that "about seventy-five small groups of people have made their homes in the most arid and crowded parts of various English and American cities, to lend a hand toward improving their neighborhoods and toward gaining a little exact knowledge of social conditions." All settlements since then have been inspired and moulded by the example of Toynbee Hall, which was erected to perpetuate the memory of this devoted young Oxfordian. "After his untimely death his friends determined to build a house in East

London where University men might live "face to face with the actual conditions of crowded city life, study on the spot the evils and their remedies, and, if possible, ennoble the lives and improve the material conditions of the people."

These social experiences have taught "all scientific reformers and apostles of light that the truth and beauty of goodness have to be lived out among the people to be understood." The social settlement to-day therefore stands for a new method of social regeneration.

"It is a social, moral, and intellectual *clearing house* and agency, where you can find and feel the social equivalent of any doctrine, new or old, of any practical or theoretical principle, new or old." It has been defined as "a group of educated men or women (or both) living among manual workers in a neighborly and social spirit." "Organized work is not essential but is a convenient method of getting acquainted. Nothing is essential except residence and a spirit of brotherhood expressed actively."

Dr. Caldwell has justly laid special emphasis upon the fact that "these settlements have come ultimately from the Universities." "It means that they are founded, not only on ideas and knowledge, but upon *personalities—*

upon the personalities of some of the finest
kind of men that are produced in Great
Britain.'' This element of personality has
always attracted the strongest class of thinkers, ''who are more willing to enter upon the
work of the education and elevation of humanity, and thereby of themselves, than upon
any other kind of service.''

Thus in this movement the social and
spiritual needs of the workers themselves have
always been kept in view. They entered
this work not in any spirit of condescension,
and not solely with the intention of bestowing
favors, but for the purpose of learning the real
facts about life, and keeping their own hearts
and minds in a healthy social balance. ''They
were to carry with them the habits and customs of culture, and by settling in congested
districts to devote themselves to the work of
common self-improvement and common elevation.''

This characteristic feature of the work
makes it an important contribution to the subject before us. It is not a mere gift, not a
surrender of privilege, not a denial of possessions, but a use of gifts, privileges, and possessions, under the direction of a spirit of
brotherhood for a common benefit. It is a
leveling up of society to the highest altitudes

of privilege, by the insistence of individual talents, tastes, and possessions.

We thus discover that the best service a man can render this community among which he has cast his lot, for the time being at least, is to be and possess something of value. Unless he is educated and refined he is of little use among the unlettered and vulgar. If he is a professional man—as physician, lawyer, or teacher—all the better. If he is a man of means and leisure, better still. "Each man has much to learn and much to teach. No rules limit his action as an individual." The movement not only gives but demands free play for all personal powers and all personal possessions. It requires a rich, full life on one side of the social and intellectual scale to make this personal service, and to such a life it returns a thousand-fold in largeness of experience, in strength of character, and in simplicity of faith.

Wealthy Christian parents are under obligation to examine this social settlement movement, not simply as a method of reformation for the submerged classes, but as a solution of the problem of self-indulgence which corrupts the moral and intellectual fiber of their own families. If they are seeking a principle of education in their civic and social duties, if they are looking for a sane method of human helpfulness, it is to be found here.

We do not say that every youth in every household of wealth must necessarily perform this service, but it is meant that along these lines of personal service are the experiences and incentives to a nobler life which is to save the youth born to means and privileges from sinking back into an unpatriotic and unchristian self-indulgence. Every age has its special problems and lessons; the youth who does not learn the lesson of his age and accept the service of his time is a degenerate. He not only fails in his own proper development, but he also deprives some other person or class of the succor which his talents and experience were intended to furnish the common good. The special lesson of our time is, that, for their own sakes, people of means and leisure must serve in their own proper persons the impoverished and the ignorant.

Thus, then, the problems of poverty, overcrowding, drink, idleness, municipal corruption, and practical atheism, which have become the disgrace and menace of our modern city life, have been attacked by the student and the lover of humanity. It is a somewhat singular fact in our modern social life that practical men, so-called, have so largely kept

aloof from this work. Philanthropists, ideal-
ists, recluses, cultured and refined women, students of social conditions—lookers-on, hitherto,
of the great drama of life—have seen the horrid
mass of pauperism increase and the breach
widen between rich and poor, and they have
at last stepped down to minister. They have
gone back to a direct imitation of Jesus. They
have reached the heart of the trouble. They
have manifested the divinity of unconscious
power, as when a child, simply because it
loves both parties, will effect a reconciliation
by taking both the disputants by the hand.

The personal service of those cultured
strong men and women is the link to bind rich
and poor together in the redeemed order of
society. What the poor and unfortunate want
is not money, but brotherhood. What the
ignorant, unpatriotic, selfish man needs is the
example of a wise, patriotic, self-sacrificing
life, lived in a place where he can see it is genuine.

What our individual use of wealth had
largely brought about was separation, more
final and hopeless than Hindu caste. Our
scholars, statesmen, men of letters, professional workers, and business men, who might
be said to carry the wealth of civilization in
the shape of brains, experience, and culture,

had become a separate class. They seldom
or never came into contact with workingmen.

Two castes have grown up in a nominal
democracy. They differ not only in material
possessions, but in ways of looking at life, in
habits of thought, and principles of action.
They need one another. The poor and ignorant citizen has a ministry for the rich and
educated. But the rich man often thought
his obligation was discharged by a dole which
the poor man returned with a curse.

Polite learning, also, in Universities had
become a recluse. Schools originally intended for the poor became the rich man's
perquisite. It became luxurious, dilletante,
and contemptuous of the *profanum vulgus.*
In Democratic America, and even in Democratic monarchies, like Great Britain, this was
the direst of political misfortunes. Political
economy, health conditions, and all those subjects which enter into a proper understanding
of wages, wealth production, and national
wellbeing, became the exclusive possession of
one class. And the class which needed them
most, as the basis of their prosperity, were left
to flounder in the mire of ignorance, or be
led into the bogs of fanaticism by demagogic
"will-o'-the-wisps."

Women of leisure, education, and refinement gave themselves so entirely to fashion and self-indulgence amid the luxuries and elegance of their homes, and to amusements, sports, and intellectual pursuits, that the gracious ministry of gentle womanhood was all but forgotten in the homes of the needy. Many of the bitterest personal sorrows and social sufferings connected with wifehood and motherhood can be understood and succored only by a wise and loving woman. Women with leisure and ability for this service were engaged in balls, routs, theatres, and house-parties, or indisposed on account of the social strain. The personal privileges of wealth had, in nominally Christian society, all but driven out the sense of its personal responsibility. Where the strain of the social system was greatest the help was feeblest or useless. The two classes, separate and frowning, faced one another, as friends who have quarreled—they stood apart "like rocks that have been rent asunder." How are these now hard, unyielding substances to be once more fused into a common nationality and common brotherhood? Only by the power of love through personal service. A right idea of the use of wealth in our Christian families will enable us to raise up a generation which will regard social service as a prince regards his heritage of government.

Towards this personal service the youth will look with interest and enthusiasm. This will be his kingdom, his privilege, his heritage, as well as his patriotic and Christian obligation. An Armenian princess, recently graduated M. D. from Berne. She has since served in the cholera hospitals of Russia, and done so much good as to receive the personal thanks of the Tsar. She is now practicing medicine at her father's palace, where sick people for miles around flock to consult her, and she is devoting a large part of her fortune to erecting an hospital to enlarge her work.

Without the possession of accumulated wealth, and consequent education and equipment, such action would be impossible. With the means, and such a wise use of it, through a rich, gracious personality, its power to corrupt the spirit of the possessor is destroyed and its ability to save and bless the people is demonstrated. It ought to be enough to say, that no condition of life can be so near an imitation of the action of Jesus and no use of money so transmute the privileges of material possessions into the immortal treasures of the soul.

XIII.

PERSONAL SERVICE A CAREER OF DISTINCTION.

A prominent public man not long since declared that the hour had come for the sons of rich men in America to give themselves, after proper equipment, to the public service simply for the honor and opportunity of doing a patriotic work. This is a most hopeful sign of the times so far as municipal and national progress is concerned. It has always been considered the most honorable, as it has proved the most glorious, phase of the history of people of rank in Europe to be able to serve their country. We need apprehend no danger from an aristocratic, exclusive, governing class in such a course of action. Our society changes too often for that. Indeed, the real danger from these changes is that we may get, not a government by the "best," but a government by the "worst."

The possession of wealth is preëminently a *prima facie* obligation to serve the State and Nation. Instead of progressing upon the

sentiments of the classic republics of the past
in this patriotic obligation, we are shamelessly
behind them.   Our rich citizens are more
anxious that their sons should continue to
trade and accumulate wealth than they are to
see them serve the City or the State as diplo-
mats and statesmen.

There is only one worse sign,—the sons too
often agree with the fathers in this.   In the
times when the free cities of Europe were the
defenders of liberty, and when Venice and
Genoa were in their glory, it was considered
an honor for a merchant to serve his native
town as alderman, mayor, provost, counselor,
or doge.   Then wealth carried with it an obligation of patriotism.   It was more honorable
to be a servant of the people than greatly
to increase the family fortune.   There can be
little hope for our Nation till this same spirit
revives in the hearts of men who are born to
wealth and privilege.

To the enlightened Christian and patriot
this should be a specially attractive field of
action for the advancement of the Kingdom
of Christ.   To give a son at the call of the
Nation for the defense of her honor in the
trying days of sixty-one, has always been regarded by loyal Americans as the greatest
proof of love of country.   But the virtue of

enlightened patriotism is as much needed in
the time of peace as in the time of war. More
indeed on the part of the wealthy, for then the
vices of luxury and materialism are more likely
to fasten on their life. The Christian man
who so regards his wealth as an opportunity to
train and equip a loyal youth for the service of
his country has made the best possible use of
his fortune, and vindicated the higher ministry
of wealth. The youth who appropriates this
ideal of service and accepts this obligation,
arising out of his education and fortune, has
proved himself the best representative of the
men of " '76" and " '61."

There is in America to-day a noble
opportunity for this service also in the work of
education. The highly educated and richly
equipped sons and daughters of our families of
wealth are sorely needed in the poor and ill-
furnished colleges of the West as instructors,
professors, and presidents. Literature and
scientific work have always been a favorite
pursuit with men of leisure and fortune. It is
within our knowledge that many men whose
fathers are engaged in commercial pursuits
have turned aside from the allurements of business to original scientific investigation, possible
only to those who can command means and
leisure. But the opportunity for young men

and women to do a great work in the moulding of the new society of the West, and at the same time find congenial avenues of action, is greatest in our educational institutions.

In such spheres there is opportunity for personal service without many of the objections attaching to it among the poor and criminal populations. That there is no remuneration, or practically none, is the greatest honor. This service to-day is rendered to the churches and to society by men and women of the most heroic self-sacrificing spirit,—men and women who had to scrape and struggle to get an education out of the hard hand of poverty. Why should the sons and daughters of wealthy Christian parents, privileged possessors of scholarship, artistic accomplishments, and refined manners, not go forth for a few of the young, strong, fresh years of their life to such work?

No interest of our American national life is so vital as the higher education of the West. It is poorly endowed, insufficiently manned, and, beyond all things, needs the personal contact of educated Eastern people. Where in all the range of philanthropic service could wealth be more fitly used than in the endowment of a Chair to which a distinguished son or daughter could give the loving, enthusiastic service of a cultured mind and a Christian heart? Is it not a wonder that the boys and girls in rich homes do not see this themselves? Or is it because in our selfish family feelings we have wished "better things" for them?

What objection could be made to such a career for the most carefully educated, sheltered, and treasured young woman? She goes among people of taste and refinement. She deals with students who are respectful, earnest, and devoted to their instructors. She will be exposed to a thousand dangers amid the ordinary amusements of society at home to one in her work in such a college. She will be honored, happy, useful, and fitted, if so desirous, for a larger life and greater service, when she chooses to return to her former home. All this is true of a son also, with this additional advantage, he will be more likely to find a field for public service and distinction in the new surroundings than in the elegant and enervating leisure, or business humdrum of conventional society life.

We must now consider a form of service particularly dear to the church, and particularly obligatory on the Christian families of to-day. By the sacredness of our profession, as well as by the genius of our religion, we stand pledged to missionary work. But how has it been done? Without doubt it offers one of the brightest pages in history. It is equally true that its half-hearted and inadequate support to-day is becoming a reproach to the Christian name.

It must get new recognition, new impulses, new attachments to our modern social forces. Its financial supporters and its actual workers are divided by social and financial considerations. The rich stay at home and give of their abundance, the poor go forth to the service as a profession. Some of the noblest and most generous rich have so found expression for their sympathy and zeal. Some of the most talented and consecrated poor have so found the happiest career of service.

But the vast increase of wealth in our Christian homes during the past hundred years has changed these conditions. Yet we are still relying on the old forces. We are in possession of a hereditary education, wealth, and moral power, as a Christian society, which did not exist when we first sent missionaries abroad, and reached our Gospel hands across the Mississippi. We have not only faith and zeal to-day, but we have cultured sons and daughters. The world needs them, and they need to bring the treasures of their lives into contact with the ignorant and the suffering at home and abroad.

The church has not yet been able to bring to bear upon the children of her own homes the constraint of love and the fascination of interest in the cause of missions which the State and education and science have used on behalf of their objects.

It is the fond and patriotic ambition of the son of wealthy parents in Britain to serve his country in India, Africa, or China, either as soldier or civil servant. When the boy goes out to this service, no mother considers it a sacrifice, no father thinks his son has acted like a fool. Yet he goes to face danger, often death. He has to be largely supplied from the parental fortune to sustain the honor of his regiment. He does not go to make money. He carries with him the old Norman spirit of roving conquest. He and his like have won for Great Britain her Colonial Empire. In these paths,—military, diplomatic, scientific, or adventure,—have been found the glory of a great service. The spirit of such men is well illustrated in General Gordon, one of the noblest of them all, who when he laid down his service in China proudly declared ''I leave China as poor as when I entered it.''

Christians of wealth and rank consider it an honor and a privilege to send their sons abroad for such a purpose.   To equip and endow a son for this service is no sacrifice, no hardship. But when it is proposed to do the same for missionary service, they reverse every principle of their former action.   Foreign service is dangerous to health; it is a great sacrifice to send the young people from home.   It is even considered a lowering of the social status; and the rich Christian father who would boast of his son's appointment to a crack regiment or a diplomatic mission would lament his ordination to a medical mission or a foreign college. Many a rich Christian mother would regard a daughter as hopelessly lost to society by taking up Zenana work in India or medical service in China; but she would be delighted to send her to either country as the wife of an officer or civil servant.   Money would cut no figure if social rank were obtained; climate would be robbed of its terrors if ''prospects'' were bright for a fashionable career.

The wealth and culture of Christians are thus looked upon as means to secure social distinction for their possessor.   And the missions of the church, as the expression of modern Christian zeal and knowledge, are deprived of the power which moves men and women in all other walks of life.   Our missionary work still rides in an oxcart while our military and

civil service rides in a Pullman car. The oxcart
has not resources enough always to procure
axle grease, while the Pullman car boasts a
perfect modern equipment, where one can
dine, read, shave, and sleep like a prince.

Sufficient funds for the vast scheme of missionary service in all its ramifications of education, medical work, evangelization, and home
influence will never be procured until the
fountain of personal interest is opened. This
can only be done by enlisting the personal
service of those who can equip and sustain ·
themselves in the wise and dutiful adoption
of a distinguished and useful career.

Already some men and women have gone
forth to service at the charge of their parents.
The people who undertake such work need
have no fear of the charge of incapacity to
sustain themselves at home. Why should
it be thought strange for a parent who will
spend $10,000 on a son's education to endow
the hospital where he goes to practice his profession with $50,000, so that his son may per-
form those services for the class, and in the
way that Jesus did?

The adoption of this principle of action
would revolutionize modern missionary service.
It would put into the field men and women
exactly fitted for special work unencumbered

by financial cares, unhindered by financial limitations.   Such men and women would necessarily be of greater breadth and scholarship
and, if the test of Moses be applied to them,
of greater spirituality and earnestness.

These self-supporting workers would command greater respect from the people among
whom they labor. The great Chinese am-
bassador who asked questions revealed the
fact that a man's social status and education
are large considerations with the heathen.
They would command the attention of the
churches, especially of our youth. The missionary would be lifted from the somewhat
doubtful category into which he has been
placed by the social notions of Christians at
home. What would some of these missionaries like Davis and Hamlin and Lawes and
Chalmers not have been able to do had they
been backed up in their work, as business men
are at home, by family fortunes? Would they
not repeat, on a greater scale, the work of the
Armenian Princess already cited? But it is
not alone the effect of such a use of Christian
wealth on the extent and character of missionary service, but the effect of it on the purity
and strength of Christianity at home, that concerns us.

What other single fact in the Christian's

experience would so enlighten, purify, and strengthen the soul as this contact with the actual progress of the Kingdom through the personal service of our most honored and privileged sons and daughters? It would draw to itself the passion of parental love, of local pride, of college honors, and of church attachment. It would open up a distinguished career for the heart and brains and privileges of our choicest youth. And it would lift Christian service at home and abroad into a position of success and distinction, which would fundamentally change our thoughts and feelings regarding it. It would prevent the calamity, fast falling upon the church, of a separate caste for Christian service. It would permit the officers of those great societies to whom we have entrusted the direction of this work to be directors and advisers of the quality and reach of statesmen; not as they are at present, collectors and dispensers of funds inadequate to the meanest scale of operations.

Above all, it would divert the attention of our disingenuous Christian youth from the deadly peril of heaping up riches for personal and family pride, which corrupt the soul as breeding-in-and-in corrupts the blood.

That such a use of Christian wealth should appear to many Utopian, reveals more clearly the vast desert of worldly conformity which separates us from a life like Paul's. We do not think it strange that a youth of rank and wealth, the gold medalist of his year and the rising hope of his party, should give up, as Paul did, all these worldly honors for Christ. But we do not expect it of our own day, and we do not educate our children with this shining example before us. It may not be amiss to remind ourselves that Paul's rank and wealth and personal equipment are declared by Professor Ramsay and the modern scholarship to be not the least important factors in the success of his marvelous career. And the distinguished place which he holds in the affections and thoughts of the Christian world is for a work more useful and a name more lasting than any he could ever have won in the service of the world.

XIV.

BUSINESS AN OPPORTUNITY OF CHRISTIAN SERVICE.

In former chapters we have considered most largely the bearing of this new ideal of wealth upon the family, education, and hereditary customs. We must now apply it to the conduct of business in the hands of a person presumably so educated and influenced.

Here, again, there is a certain fascination about schemes of profit-sharing, socialism, and other short cuts to a temporary solution of the social problem of wealth. But we have to deal with a matter of business,—not how we shall get rid of wealth to prevent spiritual injury to its possessor and to secure natural benefits to the recipient of charity, but how to make accumulated wealth in Christian hands perform the necessary functions of Capital and promote a noble Christian character? A very large proportion of Christian men must, in modern society, be engaged in commercial life; if they can not use the ideals of Christianity and lofty citizenship in this domain of business they are cut off from the realities of religion.

What considerations of the higher sort, then, can be adduced to influence a man who is in command of wealth and who prefers to remain in active business,—the man who has not the statesman's ambition, nor the necessary knowledge of art or science to permit him to take an active personal part in their advancement; the man whose faculties are still at their best, whose large knowledge of affairs and mastery of some particular business makes him a power in manufacture and commerce; the man who has made money, and still can make it, whom neither the church nor the world can afford to lose as an active factor in wealth production? Is there nothing left for such a man but to go on turning everything he touches into gold, yet finding no food in all these vast concerns for the higher cravings of the intellect and heart?

The Christian use of wealth must deal with this man's case and furnish him a method of action. This is to be discovered in the true functions of wealth itself and the true object of all commerce. Wealth is "the available thing", when it is produced the whole community flourishes. Commerce is an exchange of commodities; trade is a transaction for mutual benefits.

That there are unfortunate conditions when the product is not fairly shared, and that there is often plethora in one place and want in another, are facts outside of our present inquiry. That trade is sometimes robbery and commerce cut-throat competition is beside the point for our discussion. But that a successful business which is producing great wealth for the owners and managers of the concern is normally the condition of prosperity for the whole community is now accepted as an axiom in economics. Such a concern is a spring of water: each one may not get all he wishes or thinks he is entitled to, but if he gets any at all, he gets it from the spring; for the spring is the very condition which creates the oasis in the desert. We can deal here only with normal conditions of business to which we can apply the laws of the spiritual life.

Capital in the hands of a man who wishes to use his wealth for the higher ends of life may therefore be regarded as a power for the benefit of society. Not as philanthropy, but as business. He proposes to use his business ability for the enlargement and success of his concerns; not primarily because he is going to add thereby to his wealth, but because his business so conducted is the material basis of the prosperity of a whole community. This is no dream, but already a fixed principle in the life of some business men. Nor is it without charm for many minds of the larger calibre. If we will call to mind the large part which the inventive genius, the careful business management, the mastery of commercial conditions play in the production of wealth, we shall see that this service is of immense value to the community. These men are the captains of industry, leaders in new enterprises, brain-workers who give useful direction to the productive manual labor of others. The annals of modern industry are crowded with illustrations of this fact. Such inventions as Whitney's cotton gin, Salt's alpaca weaving, Corliss' engine, McCormick's reaper, Morse and Vail's telegraphic systems, S. Gilchrist Thomas' elimination of phosphorus, and the Edison electric appliances advanced the wealth of the world by leaps and bounds.

"Sir Lowthian Bell, who writes with the highest authority, says that the annual 'get' of Cleveland stone alone contained an amount of phosphorus which if released would be worth £250,000 ($1,250,000), but which as an ingredient diminished the annual value by £4,000,-000 ($20,000,000)."* This problem of wealth was solved by S. G. Thomas, and by his in-

* "Wealth and Wages"—papers by the author.

vention alone $21,500,000 per year was pro-
duced at the outset. Similar illustrations of
the part played by the management of great
concerns abound on every hand. Thus to be
able to increase the efficiency of natural forces
by invention, to master commercial conditions,
to prevent waste by careful management, to
create wealth in a word, as a general wins
battles, has as great a fascination as statesmanship or conquest.

With the various economic plans by which
the wealth so created shall be best distrib-
uted among the people, whether by ordinary
wages, co-operation, or what not, it is not
necessary for us to deal. This will depend
entirely upon the local conditions of the owners and laborers, upon character, skill, permanence of residence, and trade customs, which
entirely govern such questions. It is sufficient
to know that even by the ordinary wage system
some seventy-five per cent. of all created wealth
goes to the manual worker; that the proportion
going to capital, management, and invention is
continually growing smaller, and that going to
the manual laborer continually growing larger.
It is only by corrupt and illegal interference
with the laws of trade and by personal and
local vice on the part of owners or workers in
industrial concerns that this law is hindered.

But a concern conducted for such high ends as in the case supposed by us will increase the proportion rather than diminish it, even when no extraordinary or special schemes are adopted. Where, however, such a spirit prevails in the operation of great business enterprises, all practical and just plans for the better sharing of products will be welcomed and fostered. This also brings its own commercial reward, and such concerns as can be run on lines of profit-sharing have frequently resulted in greater accumulations of wealth. They result also in what is of greater value to the social and religious life,—in more intelligent, more skilled, and more virtuous workmen.

Such a purpose in business makes the desert rejoice and blossom as the rose. It must be observed in estimating the value of this ideal of business, that it demands for its success the possession of accumulated wealth, not merely in the form of capital to be used in the business, but the family heritage which has come in the shape of education and the start in life. In the case of men who have accumulated wealth in their own lifetime so regarding business at a later period in their career there is no real exception to the principle. If it has not operated on them in the way here supposed it will on their children, whom they instruct and inspire.

Again we are to observe that it permits the full normal operation of business principles in the accumulation of wealth, it limits nothing, it denies nothing, it interferes with no right in personal property, and it demands no self-denying ordinance from the man in the prime of life. It is possible such a man may regard his ability to conduct a successful business as the only means by which he can serve God and society. It is possible also he detests and dreads all forms of mere charity. What he wants to do for the benefit of others is to furnish work: to open the mills, the forges, the shipyards; to develop the natural resources of the mine, the field, the forest. If so he is a very close imitator of the best rulers, ancient or modern. There is more statesmanship, more religion, in such an ideal of business, than in half the laws and half the sermons.

The proudest boast of a prince is that he is the shepherd and judge of his people. The best government is that which spreads prosperity and fosters manhood. All these virtues are compacted in such an ideal and method of business. Nor is its operation confined to great concerns: its spirit can be manifested on the humblest scale.

It is not necessary for a man to put off doing good in this way until he has grown rich himself. It is very likely such an one will never feel its constraint. Few people grow generous as they grow old. The men of public spirit and large philanthropy felt the impulse and generously responded to it in youth. So we must look to teaching our youth this nobler meaning and sacred obligation of wealth in business.

If it should be charged against such an ideal by the practical man that it is visionary and unnatural; that the motive which impels men in business is purely selfish,—we can only reply: "Granted that it is so largely; yet there are some noble exceptions." The end of all higher teaching is to make the exception the rule, to turn the minority into a majority. This is the way all reforms have been wrought, many of them far harder of accomplishment than this.

But the case in support of this ideal is even better. There are conspicuous instances where such use of wealth is the dominant principle in life. The owner of one of the large fortunes in America has recently proved himself the possessor of ideas of public utility as well as personal ambition which furnish us an example of this service on a large scale. His estate of ninety-five thousand acres is being used to show what scientific cultivation can do. The Secretary of Agriculture reports concerning this domain: "That he had seen the most perfect system of roadways, an exhibition of landscape-gardening that cannot be paralleled, and buildings which for dwellings, stables, barns, dairies, propagating houses, henneries, and other uses surpass everything within his knowledge." He declared this great experiment as important to the agricultural interests of this country as the Federal Department of Agriculture at Washington. "This wealthy citizen employs more men than I have under my charge. He is spending more money every year than Congress appropriates for the Agricultural Department of the Nation. His men are promoted for efficiency according to the most practical civil-service rules. He is building up an educational institution that will be of the greatest value to scientific farmers and teachers for the instruction of others in domestic architecture, agriculture, forestry, viticulture, dairying, roadmaking, and other useful sciences. It is one of the grandest undertakings that individual enterprise ever attempted; and I understand," the Secretary concludes, "that it is the owner's intention to leave it as a legacy to the public."

It may be urged regarding the above illustration that this is not a business concern in the usual acceptance of that term, but an educational experiment. As such the question of profit does not enter into it; and unless the owner possessed large means he would be unable to sustain it.

This makes the instance of the greater importance to our particular enquiry. We want to know if any normal, unrestricted, and sane use of large wealth accumulated in the hands of one person can be made of benefit both to the possessor and the community, for we are assured that the man thus using his wealth is most certainly safeguarded from the deterioration of character and the infidelity of spirit called worldly conformity. In the above instance, however, it would be exaggeration to say the experiment was not conducted on strict business principles, each part productive and the whole a financial success.

Now as an illustration of our subject we have to notice that such a work, at once of vast public benefit to the immediate employees and to the general community, could not be undertaken nor sustained without a vast accumulation of wealth. Nor could it be used in this way under any principle of restriction, deprivation, or denial of the right of personal property. The virtue then, whatever it is, both personal and communal, arises from the successful accumulation of wealth in the first instance.

In addition, however, it is an ideal use of wealth; it includes the idea of stewardship, personal ownership, and personal service; it is the putting of the owner's thought, feeling, interest, and fellowship into a business concern. It is therefore altruism in business, based upon the firm ground of common interest in productive occupations. The field for character, virtue, public and personal, is thus occupied in such action.

The social and business inducements to work in this way are natural. They are susceptible of appreciation, it is true, only by those who have high ideals and a deep sense of responsibility, but they are in the line of sanity, nature, and education. They are such as the more spiritual interpretation of the Christian use of wealth is continually calling for from all the followers of Jesus. They may not be set aside either as impractical or without obligation. More or less, they are of deep and permanent obligation on all. And it is as this principle of business action, this ideal of personal service through wealth, enters into all commercial and professional life, that

it is saved from the taint of mere self-seeking
and raised to the dignity of human fellowship.
It would remove the canker from many a
manly spirit corrupting with the sordidness of
business; it would open new visions of the
possibilities of wealth, and save it from the
terrible indictment, made too often with truth,
that its possession is a curse, both to the possessor and the community.

Reformers are not without hope that in
these latter days, in a commercial community
where the possession of inherited wealth and
the native capacity for business mark men
out as leaders of their fellows, such men
will undertake the social obligations of wealth
and elect to serve the public in the leadership
of commerce, education, civic affairs, and religion.

Nature has no mercy on those who break
her laws.   The forces which might bring
health and the divinest exhilaration if used
at the right time and place and for their
proper purpose, bring disease and bitter suffering when misapplied.   Wealth is a force of
nature, the store-chamber of a thousand other
forces.   Congested in our heart, the elements
which should fructify a province will destroy
like a pestilence.   Misused for our life or our
family, the treasures which should reach the

homes of thousands will be millstones to sink the self-seekers into the depth of the sea.

With such a business ideal and use of wealth the owner enters into partnership with Nature, secures her beneficent operation, and sees her forces multiply a thousand-fold for the benefit of the whole community. He makes Nature the servant and promoter of moral qualities also in the realization of a brotherhood of business and the victory of his own spirit over these vices of mere possession and gratification.

Christians will never really know what secrets of moral and spiritual dynamics are stored up in wealth for a civilized community until such ideals unloose them, as Faraday and Thomson have set free the energies of Nature. Nay, they will never know the productive power of accumulated wealth, the real possibilities of capital, until this moral energy be applied in business. The virtues and affections of man as vital forces for the creation of wealth and the spread of civilization are more potent in business than muscle or brain. These are only partly utilized as yet The man who regards his business primarily in the light of a service for God and men, is revealing the secrets and setting free the forces of matter and spirit for the purification and enrichment of life.

XV.

THE PERSONAL ADMINISTRATION OF ACCUMULATED WEALTH.

In certain parts of Great Britain, endowments of educational and other institutions are called "mortifications." Death, one can see, is plainly written on the face of the word. It reminds us that almost all gifts from private persons to the public were legacies that could be realized only when the testator had passed away. There are many reasons, in the nature of the case, why public benefactions and even private inheritances must be of this character. Lear's calamity is not an impossible one to-day; and there will always be cases where accumulated wealth can not be wisely disposed of till the death of the owner and the satisfaction of his heirs.

But certainly in the vast majority of instances, especially in modern times, wealth which is ultimately intended for a public gift can be bestowed during the life of the owner. Then one of the noblest emotions of the human spirit can be felt by the giver. Then one of the most unique of services can be rendered by one man to his fellows—he can administer upon his own estate. He can not only live in his own child as a father, in his own book as an author, but he can erect his own monument and animate his own statue.

This method of the disposal of wealth is becoming common among the most intelligent public benefactors of our time. Even now, in the West, there are conspicuous examples of men still managing their business concerns for the purpose of having fresh resources to administer. Some of the most munificent public gifts of our times are of this character. In this connection the names of Drexel, Pratt, Childs, Wanamaker, Ford, Armour, Pearsons are readily remembered. The practice will certainly grow in favor, for it appeals to those business qualities which have made their possessors successful.

What satisfaction is found in toiling for life and accumulating wealth which the foolish or vicious or incapable may dissipate or turn to the confusion of the giver's memory? Why bestow a benefaction that may be grossly perverted? At least for many years of the best part of the giver's life the same powers which went to making the fortune may be used to conserve it to the high ends for which it is

designed. Besides all this, the modern instances, in which the notorious intention of
the testator has been frustrated by legal tech-
nicalities, have made men of wealth feel that
the best will is one executed in the testator's
lifetime.

The personal administration in philanthropy
of accumulated wealth is, therefore, one of
the most conspicuous ways of rendering social
service and at the same time saving the owner
from the spirit of worldliness. It singles out
in the most conspicuous way his personality.
It proposes no interference with his tastes or
his device in the disposal of what is entirely
his own. It does what Nature has already
done, just reminds him, that if he would
really possess it he must use it; that if he
would own its nobler qualities, he must give it
away. It reminds him that wealth corrupts,
rusts, may be stolen in possession, but is in-
vincible and immortal if returned to the public
use.

Now we are concerned with the effect of
such a method of beneficence on the mind
and heart of the possessor principally. In the
ordinary gift of a Christian to missions or a
public-spirited citizen to institutions of learning or city adornment we presuppose generosity, interest in the objects benefited, and a

certain magnanimity or patriotism. Gratitude to the community where the wealth has been made, and local pride from birth and early avocations, play also a not unimportant part in large benefactions. Such motives have been regarded in all ages and countries among Christians as worthy of our faith and expressive of our noblest aims in life. Under the impulse of such aims men have been known to live soberly, industriously, and with great self-sacrifice, that in the end they might confer upon the public some large and lasting memorial of their name and gratitude.

To some extent, therefore, all legacies for public service ennoble wealth. The intention anticipates a consecration of means to a worthy purpose; but it is not the most truly indicative of the higher uses of wealth.

These are inseparably allied to personal service and administration. When, therefore, the benefactor gives during his lifetime, and takes a personal share in the direction of the objects he is endowing, he becomes a fellow-worker in the higher service. Such an administrator may not be an artist, yet he may see with his own eyes some great masterpiece which his wealth helped to create. He may not be an astronomer or physicist, yet he may learn the secrets of Nature which his wealth helped to lay bare. He may not be a preacher, yet he may see the man redeemed, sitting clothed and in his right mind, which his wealth helped to regenerate. He may not be a physician, yet he may look into the grateful eyes of those who have got healing and strength in the hospital which his wealth founded. Nay, he may make the greatest of all human boasts, and that too in a spirit of praise rather than boastfulness. He may say "These things I not only aided with money, but indeed part of these achievements I was"; thus his *pars fui* will have a grander meaning than the statesman's or historian's. He becomes not only a munificent patron, but a helper and fellow-worker in the intellectual and spiritual creations of which his wealth is the material basis.

Here then is a vital social and economical force in action among the most intensely interesting of all human concerns. Such men as feel its charm and are inspired in their life work by it, will reap its richest fruits in the development of their own best powers. They will see as never before the higher ministry of wealth: its varied services in the mitigation of human suffering, the dissipation of ignorance, the spread of truth and purity, the advancement of art, literature, and science, the elevation of the common lot, the adornment of cities, and the progress of civilization in all its forms.

To such men and to their families the more personal uses of wealth will assume a secondary significance. Do we anticipate family disaffection as the result of such a disposition of wealth beyond the direct control of the family? I saw recently the daughter of a man of large wealth, who had made a gift to a public institution, sitting in one of the classes, listening with delighted face, and herself a worker in the settlement which her father's money had endowed. Instead of quarrels and selfishness in a home where this spirit and method is adopted we might expect more such sons and daughters, themselves honored and interested workers in the institutions which perpetuate a noble parent's name. What purer pleasure, what nobler ambition in life can we possibly conceive than such a fellowship in interest and work between the wise, strong father, whose industry and genius have won the wealth, and the intelligent, cultured sons and daughters who are glad to share in its disposal of such high ends?

When some great life story is laid bare for us in a true biography, we are frequently startled by the revelation of human pity and magnanimity shown by a noble merchant prince in the use of his wealth for some institution where a dearly loved son or daughter can take a personal share of the management or minor service. Such experiences are the nectar of the gods, nay let us rather say the earnest of the spiritual fellowship of heaven, where the service of congenial spirits for congenial objects is the very fruition of the soul.

We need fear no lack of interest in the spread of the Gospel of Christ where such a plan of life prevails. We need anticipate no foolish, vain display, no waste, no luxury, no indifference to the appeal of the needy and the ignorant, where such a principle rules. We need dread no more the ambition which destroys the early zeal of the Christian worker, no luxury which puts to shame our Christian simplicity—nothing, in a word, which sows the fatal seed of conformity in the rank soil of unconsecrated riches.

Ruled by such ideas we would find a deeper sense of personal responsibility for the improvement of all intellectual and moral qualities making the rich man and his family more fit to share in this higher service. By coming in contact with men and women of ideas and spirituality, they would respond naturally to the ideal and spiritual in their whole life. Things of the intellect and spirit which the wealthy and fashionable disregard would become real and familiar. The fatal cycle would be broken. The forces of disintegration would be arrested. Money which breeds the maggots of ennui, enervation, and disgust, when used for mere selfish indulgence, begets zest, strength, and hope when put to the higher service.

Such magnanimous men and such homes would be the centres of new social and educational forces: they would occupy the places which the Mæcenases, the Medici, Wolseys, Heriots, Harvards, and Shaftsburys have occupied in the past, only with new and more tender personal relationships, as befit the changed spirit of the times. "Honor to whom honor is due," is one of the exhortations of Scripture. There would be no disposition in the heart of a grateful people to withhold the meed of praise to lives so consecrated to public service.

The new philanthropy may expect to see a new race of patrons of art, science, literature, and social reform; a new class of public benefactors for the relief of suffering, the enrichment of public life, and the solution of the civic problems of our time should this purpose of personal service in the administrations of their wealth once possess the heart of intelligent Christians. For the Christian man charged with the bestowal of large means, it is one of the surest tests of the real sincerity of his spirit and one of the most splendid opportunities for the achievement of a great destiny.

XVI.

THE FAMILY INHERITANCE.

The strongest instinct of nature, as in the case of the mother, superseding even personal preservation, is the preservation of offspring. This instinct has been sanctified in religion so that it occupies a place next to the salvation of one's own soul. It might weigh with one more than one's own salvation, as it did with the Apostle Paul. It has been made much of here by implication, for it lies at the basis of the teaching — ''But if any provideth not for his own, and especially his own household he hath denied the faith and is worse than an unbeliever.''

This sentiment lies at the foundation of all the laws of primogeniture and entail which built up the power of feudalism in Europe. It is practically the force which dominates all family life to-day in Europe and America. The feudal chief associated family permanence, by a wise foresight, with the possession of land. A family, like an idea, if it is to come to anything, needs ''a local hab-

itation and a name." The European conqueror early possessed himself of the land of
the conquered. He built his castle and his
manor, and took root in the soil. He became
a great tree, drinking sap and vigor from the
soil and air of the locality.

He did not disdain to increase his family
fortune by alliances and by commerce directly
or indirectly, for the noble was not unwilling
then, as now, to sell a title for money. If
blood could not make money, money could
buy blood. The family inheritance was a
vital necessity. Great names have perished
from the peerage because the family fortune
has been lost. Great names to-day are with-
held from the golden book because the fortunes of the owners are not considered sufficient to sustain a peerage. When a commoner
is raised to the peerage in Britain he must
have an estate from which to derive his title.
A landless lord is a reproach of the bitterest
sort.

When men make money in trade, their
first step in the social ladder is the purchase
of land. To be John Smith of Broadacres
is the first indication to the public that the
wealthy ironmaster or brewer has social ambitions. A territorial title is the greatest passion of the European to-day, as it has been

for the last thousand years. Even the farmer, at least in Scotland, is called by the name of his farm. It is not "John Baxter," but "Burnbrae,"—the name of the farm— which marks his place in the social scale.

There is much sense, much Anglo-Saxon tenacity in this territorial instinct. It has made the European a man of the place— given him *locus standi* among his neighbors, and tenants, and retainers. His duties, his sports, his honors were on his estate. His great energies, his conquering forces were bred and nourished close to the soil. He became like his own oaks and elms in the parks of Europe, the beautiful and dominating feature of the landscape. Like all great creatures he had a place; like the eagle he bred his brood in the same nest, and if he preyed upon the flock he also added majesty to the terrestrial scene. This attachment to place, to the old nest, to the home of one's ancestors, is a mark of the strongest and finest natures.

Its disappearance in American life is one of the greatest defects of our age. Here the city swallows up all interests. Even the "old homestead" is deserted and sold for a little capital to start life in the city. Children born to the privilege of a grand "old homestead," associated either with colonial or early western experiences, should cherish it as the most precious possession of life. No more certain signs of deterioration in the East and South can be found than the careless desertion of the old home.

Commercial men to-day in our American cities will sell anything to turn a dollar. The old cradle, the home where the children were born, and where grandma died, they are only chattels to be knocked down to the highest bidder. Families change their residences on the merest whim. They are here to-day and away to-morrow like birds of passage.

The children have no holy associations about home places, they are robbed of all contact with Nature, and the spirit of reverence for the past dies out like a forgotten song. The peasantry of Europe and the farmers of America are the backbone of their respective nationalities principally because they grow strong with the lime and iron of the soil; they are rooted and grounded in the primal and natural home places where deep intellects and strong frames are reared.

The relation of these instincts and these social customs to the family inheritance is strong and direct. We see that a family inheritance is a natural, wise, religious provision.

Men who love their family will toil and save for their sake. They will seek the means of protecting their weak and dependent ones from the rude buffets of poverty. No greater horror can come upon a wise, tender father and husband than the thought of leaving wife and daughters unprovided against his death, and exposed to the pitiless shafts of poverty. A writer makes one of his characters say, in a letter to his daughter about his will, "The Lord has prospered me, and there is more than enough for you and your mother all your days. And that thought gives me peace, for it is an ill thing to see women wrestling with the world." No person of fine feelings will fail to see the naturalness and propriety of this paternal sentiment.

In considering, therefore, the bearing of the family inheritance on individualism and worldly conformity, we lay it down as a fundamental principle in religion and Nature, that provision for the family wellbeing and perpetuation are prime considerations. Anything that would weaken this claim of the family upon the provider must be condemned as pestilent and vicious. The members of a family born and reared in a position of affluence and culture have rights arising from this condition of birth and education. The parents will set the son up in business, provide the daughter a dower, invest funds for his or her particular needs if personal infirmity demand that form of provision.

This principle of action is so strongly felt that no person of wealth will adopt a child, rear him or her in comfort and educate them for a higher sphere, and then leave them unprovided for. Such conduct would be regarded as little less than criminal. The instincts of nature, the common sense of men, the tender love of the Christian heart may all be relied upon to secure the protection of the family and the proper provision for one's own required by Scripture.

But the moral bearing of the family inheritance on modern Christian society has assumed quite another phase from this. Not even in the matter of worldly amusements has the Christian man who is being corrupted by the world, so openly adopted the principles of the world as in the creation of family fortunes. The ambition of the vast majority of Christian men seems to be to pile up vast wealth to leave to children and even more distant heirs. Every day brings its tale of disaster to such men. They die in harness. They are spent before their time. They toil and struggle to amass more and more to leave to

some one who shall come behind. The Psalmist gave it as a mark of the worldling, they
"leave the rest of their substance to their
babes." But now it is the Christian who
makes this his one aim in life. The great
mass of wealth accumulated in modern times
in Europe and America has been accumulated
by nominally Christian men. But more and
more it is bequeathed to heirs to be held in
perpetuation of family names and estates.

A large part of such wealth, in more recent
times, by some startling phases of social life,
is going over from America to Europe to re-
build the fallen fortunes of the nobility.
What remains at home here is affected by the
feudal taint. The European noble was candid
and open in his methods to build up great
houses. He invented the laws of primogeniture, of entail, of hypothec, of game, and
all the other class privileges of the rich to
secure for the head of the house riches and
power.

We can not make such laws in America,
but we are copying social customs concerning
family inheritances equally as effective for the
destruction of democratic simplicity and equality. Surely a sober second thought will show
us how vain all this is, how destructive of all
the higher ideas of Christianity, and how fatal

even to commercial success, in our society, such a course becomes.

Perhaps we ought to dismiss those instances where the parents, in utter forgetfulness of their own professions of Christian faith and spiritual ideals, rear their children in fashionable luxury, among idle companions, with no thought of the obligations of wealth, and allow them to look forward to the time when all the accumulated wealth of years shall fall into their hands to be used as they please. But such instances are so numerous that they demand the attention of the thinker and lover of good society. This is the extreme case; but it is symptomatic of the general practice of the wealthy Christians of our age. In such a case the parent allows wealth which God has given him as the fruit of years of labor and the product of Christian virtues to be deflected from its natural course of benevolence and perverted to the most vicious private ends. What if the person so misusing the wealth is one's child. What if the time is many years after the parent has gone from earth. Was there no obligation to see that such wealth should fall into proper hands to be used for noble purposes?*

---

* Since writing these words, a will has been made public which contains a very remarkable vindication of

But even in those cases where the members of the family adopt their parents' faith and spiritual ideals, have children any right to expect a parent to toil and scramble and exhaust every power of body and mind, merely to add a few thousands more to the family fortune? Are men wise to put such a premium on their own death? What object is served for the social advancement, the business success, or the Christian virtue of a child when a parent leaves him several millions rather than the simple capital of his business or the modest legacy that remains out of what he expected to need for his own uses? The children's rights have, supposedly, in every intelligent Christian family been already regarded. They have been well born, well educated, well trained to commerce or the professions, or to public service. They are companions with their parents in business or social service. That part of the family fortune which is invested in business or the funds or other commercial concerns, they have their share in, present and

the principle here advanced for the determination of the family inheritance. This testator discards the feudal principle of primogeniture in the male line, and substitutes personal fitness on moral and intellectual grounds.

It is not a long step from such action to the recognition of the principle that, not ties of blood, but bonds of the spirit constitute the rights of heirship to a Christian man's wealth.

prospective. But what right have they to look for other, vaster, and still further accumulations, which will require continued toil and business slavery from their honored and loved father?

Of course they have none. Perhaps they are most eager for their father to call a halt, to enter with them into the enjoyment of and higher uses of what has already been secured. Recently we were called to mourn the loss of a business man, some fifty years of age, who had within the past few years amassed in a most honorable commercial career a great fortune. He was a leader in our missionary and philanthropic work, not simply as a giver but as a personal worker. He was a man of family in the prime of life. He was a wise counselor and a director of our Christian interests. But he would not rest; he would not content himself with what he had already won. He still wanted more; Pelion on Ossa piled high. But alas for family, for church, for public interest, they had to lay him away in an untimely grave!

Is not the very essence of the Christian life lost in such a career? Time that should be spent in the home, in intellectual and spiritual pursuits with the family, and a life that might have been long spared to the public service are

ruthlessly sacrificed to family greed and ambition. He loses his life literally by seeking to
save it; he gains the whole world only to
lose his own soul.

Aye, dreadful as the thought may be, such
a father can never be sure, even when he
looks into the eyes of those dearest to him,
but that some demon of covetousness, whom
his own worldliness has begotten, may lurk
behind the countenance of his child. May
there not arise a wish to have the "old man"
away that the heir may possess and enjoy.
The iron entered the soul of Earl Gloster
when he thought his son Edgar had written "If our father should sleep till I waked
him you should enjoy half of his revenue for-
ever"; for as the father said, the ingratitude
was unnatural "to his father that so tenderly
and entirely loves him, Heaven, and Earth!"
Yet it is the tendency of our habits, as it
was, in this case, the infection of the times,
to breed such unnatural vices.

Such conduct is foolish even from a commercial point of view—the expectation of
great riches is so often fatal to study, industry, and character. Society is strewn with
the wrecks of men who might have been great
and happy but for inherited wealth, or even
its expectation. One of the greatest author-

ities on modern business and on American social tendencies says: "It would be well for the lesson to be enforced upon the students of your University that the ranks of success in business and the professions are not recruited from the sons of the rich, but almost entirely from the field of workers."* If then a continued success in business or a great career in the professions is the aim of a fond parent, it may be laid down as a certain rule—"Do not leave your boy a fortune."

There are many sociological reasons to be rendered for hereditary fortunes in old countries, where they invariably go with great estates; for the estate has tenants, and the obligations of great wealth are more readily recognized in such a case. The nobleman or gentleman neglectful of his social and moral responsibility in his parish is considered a dishonor and a danger to his order. But in America only the personal privileges belonging to great inherited wealth are likely to present themselves. There are no tenantry, no dependent peasantry, no social parish obligations that rest upon the "lord of the manor."

In the social life of America hereditary fortunes are dissociated from all those humanities which tend to keep them sweet and

* Dr. Chauncey M. Depew, in a public letter.

pure. They are provocative of self-indulg-ence, a hindrance to the natural career of the American citizen, and separate him further and further from the people. We must recon-sider this whole subject of family inheritances from every point of view, as Christians, busi-ness men, and citizens of this great Republic.

Its relation to our present enquiry is very plain and very important. The Christian man who imperils his own spiritual interests and sacrifices his own higher service to the family and the State in amassing wealth for the sake of leaving a family fortune, is recreant to every principle of religion, false to every experience of education and every duty of American citizenship. Unrelated to what has been said about the Christian education of the family and the personal service of men of means, this might appear to be a contradiction of one of the main positions of our theme—the power of wealth in social service,—but as the logical result of the wise use of riches, the obligation of personal service, and the administration of wealth while the giver lives, it will be seen to be a consistent outcome of the whole teaching of this work.

We know that neither the happiness, the honor, nor the usefulness of our children de-pend upon the vastness of the family inherit-

ance.   Every one of those interests and ambitions which make a Christian family noble and
happy would be advanced a thousand-fold by
the just administration of the wealth during
the lifetime of the owner.   If the unreasoning
instinct to leave money to a child, without regard to character, ideals of life, and use to
which the wealth may be put, is to be accepted by Christians as a paramount obligation,
then the strongest passion of the worldling is
the dominant force in Christian society.

Did we understand the higher uses of wealth,
no such parental folly would be possible:
it would be considered a reproach for a Christian man to pile up a vast fortune to gratify
family pride, and leave it under control of
anti-Christian ideals of life.   The Christian
ideal would be to use wealth as it was earned
in the education of the family, in their settlement in life, in fitting and endowing them for
positions of honorable service, and in the administration of the surplus wealth upon objects
which claimed the sympathies and co-operation of both parents and children.

The children would thus be partners both
in the business and benevolence of the parents.
They would be sharers in the comforts, the
honors, the privileges, and ideals of their life.
Their wealth would accumulate as much in

moral power and usefulness as in material increase. They would perpetuate an ideal of
life, a principle of service, a sort of moral dy-
nasty which should give permanence and
splendor to their name. One of the strongest
anti-Christian passions of the ages would be
met by "the expulsive power of a new affection."

Wealth would no longer be an end in itself,
but a means to the noblest of all ends. In its
accumulation it would take a new character
and gather new force, because of what it could
be made to do in the hands of such possessors.
Family ambition would not consist in a contin-
uous approximation to fashionable and worldly
examples, but would be in the perpetuation of
great Christian traditions. *Noblesse oblige*, in
the new order of society, would be the watchword of those who, possessing culture, and
faith, and wealth, used their possessions in the
grace of gentlehood and the dignity of service,
because they had learned the secret of that
saying "He that is greatest among you let
him be your servant."

XVII.

THE NEW CHRISTIAN CIVILIZATION.

What Christians need to-day is a divine passion for righteousness in the civilization of their age and nation. Some are wise, dignified, intellectual: others are earnest, spiritual, and generous: while a happy third mingle these gracious traits in healthy proportions. But there is a conspicuous absence of fire and abandon of soul in the interests of some over-mastering passion or in pursuit of some fascinating ideal. There is much sense, but little poetry, in the average Christian's life.

We hear some of the demands made by Jesus on the Christian heart as if they belonged to a world of dreams and He the splendid dreamer. There is no predominant conception of life and duty in the Christianity of our day forcing all its intellectual, spiritual, and material forces into an energy which will carry the church to certain conquest over the forces of evil in the society around her. We have no dominant creative ideal concerning the nature and purpose of the civilization which,

consciously or unconsciously, we are moulding. We are comfortable, satisfied with
things as they are, if we are fairly successful in
life. We are "lapped in soft Lydian airs,"
perhaps "sunk in Capuan languors." We
have not the strenuous note, the spirit of
heroes, the devotion of martyrs, the consecration of Saints.

There is a most alarming and suggestive
contrast between the listless tone of the average Christian and the quickening enthusiasm
of the various secular interests of life. Science carries its votaries off their feet with a
whirlwind of zeal for the investigation of the
secrets of nature. Work—eager, incessant,
triumphant—is the watchword of the new
studies ranging from the worm to the stars.
Literature is a teeming hive of earnest, seri-
ous, highly-equipped workers; and there is
a spirit, a tang, a snap, a zest of life in all they
say and sing. Commerce also, even if fevered
and overstrained, is energetic and command-
ing, calling forth some of the most splendid examples of creative intellectual activity in our
time. It has passed into a proverb concerning
the artist, that he becomes a slave to the fascinations of art. Statesmanship is but another name for the most consuming ambitions.
In all these realms we detect the note of real-

ity, the keen delight of the warrior, conscious of a noble cause and animated by the firm conviction of a successful issue, the transport of the prophet and poet under the spell of a lofty vision and the inspiration of a noble ideal.

Such was the spirit of the first Christians in their efforts for social redemption. To regain this strenuous note of life, to re-possess this heroic spirit, the Christian must learn anew his obligation to society, his debt to the spiritual claims of civilization. In doing so we will run no risk of forgetting our obligation to the individual, for the individual claim has already been met, and out of it has sprung this new obligation.

We must reconstruct our Christian doctrine of life in its totality under the pressure and in the light of the social needs and teachings of our own time. Besides the individual, society must be regarded as the subject of salvation; for though the individual soul creates society, in turn society reacts upon the individual.

The end of religion is a perfect civilization. Sin exists in and pollutes the soul of society just as truly as it exists in and pollutes the individual soul. The curse of sin, thus considered, is its power to destroy. It limits, deprives, destroys all wealth, whether of souls or bodies. And because it pulls down and destroys civilization and the fruits of man's toil, physical and intellectual, it is thereby a destroyer of souls.

The Christian thinker must come, therefore, to see that an ignorant, narrow, poor, social life is a degradation of our Christian manhood and a destroyer of souls. This is only another way of saying that intemperance, unthrift, avarice, license, and injustice are rivers of death, which swell the great sea of human misery to the mockery and confusion of the Gospel of Jesus.

The Christian requires a social ideal for the work of to-day which will give him the accent of conviction, the fire of a generous love, and "put life into the very ribs of death:" otherwise we cannot escape the charge that our Gospel is no exception to the universal law of nature which reveals "the world as struggling with all its force for the destruction of what it has itself brought forth."

Must we then accept this judgment of pessimism, and read the doom of our dearest spiritual hopes in the failure of the Gospel to regenerate society? Does Christianity, like all world forces, "weave her own shroud and pile up the stones of her own tomb"? At all events she will be tested by the kind of civilization she produces; for this is the spiritual atmosphere which her own children are compelled to breathe, in which they must think and work, and win their crown or meet their fate.

If Christian parents should be content to let their children be born in dirt and squalor, be reared among the vagabonds and vicious, and intermarry with the criminal and unchaste, they would be denounced as apostate and unnatural. Yet the Christian churches of Europe and America let the souls committed to their care in large sections of the community be so born, reared, and married, and it does not appear to them unnatural or absurd.

There is apparently a wide separation between the rich, cultured Christian who lives in the repose and refinement of his suburban villa, and the thugs, criminals, and outcasts who herd in the conjested districts of our great cities; but there is no real separation of fate, so far as history teaches us. When the atmosphere is poisoned with the deadly small-pox and diphtheria there is an equal danger to the children in the castle and the children in the hut. When a ship catches fire, the same fate awaits the millionaire in the salon as the pauper in the steerage; captain and cabin-boy are on an equal footing in the hour of common danger.

The Christian church will get back from society what she gives to society. By virtue of our very faith in the social energy of Christianity we are compelled to admit that with what measure we mete it shall be measured to us again. If, then, this civilization which Christianity has done so much to create, and which, in its turn, becomes the soil in which Christian graces are to grow and flourish, has not yet yielded us much fruit, it is simply because we have neglected the teachings of our Lord and defied the laws of the human soul.

Philosophers say that Christian humanity is not much better than Pagan humanity. This assertion might be set aside as a prejudice, and the contrary successfully maintained, but it clearly proves that the condition of humanity as a whole, and not separate atoms here and there in favored places, is the supreme test of the value of the Christian gospel. A small pump will raise the level of the water in a village pond, but only elemental forces approaching the supernatural will raise the level of the ocean. Civilization is an ocean. The changes in its character and spirit require the operation of elemental forces approaching the supernatural. We must grant either an infinite duration of time for the action of small persistent forces or an infinite energy exercised by some great force instantaneously, if we hope to change great interests like society.

It sometimes happens that these two kinds of forces are combined and act together. Christianity, as the quickener of the individual soul and the reformer of social life, should be used so as to bring to bear all her regenerative powers upon the forces of civilization. Christianity, as the religion of the new birth and of eternal life, is an elemental moral force. Wealth, as the evidence of strong personality and productive energy, is an elemental material force. The one is an evidence in the world of an elemental spiritual power which strikes with infinite energy instantaneously, and yet persists, through generation after generation, moulding, inspiring, and creating civilized life after its own image: the other is an evidence in the world of an elemental physical power which will strike as instantaneously and with infinite energy, and it, too, persists, through generation after generation, to work weal or woe in the Christian civilization where it has been used. If these forces, the spiritual and the physical in the Christian economy, are divorced and rendered antagonistic by false or unworthy ideals of life, they will become mutually destructive of the higher civilization which the Saints and seers of the church have ever aimed to create. If they are wedded in a noble ideal of life, rendered sympathetic and mutually helpful, they become the parents of a divinely perfect human society.

The economist says, "The odd thing about wealth is the small impression the preachers and moralists have ever made about it. From the very earliest times its deceitfulness, its inability to produce happiness, its fertility in temptation, its want of connection with virtue, have been among the commonplaces of religion and morality."* Thus even on economic grounds the demand is made that wealth shall be spent under the direction of moral ideas.

True, the luxury and display of the pagan world, as seen in the lives of Hadrian, Lucullus, and Mæcenas, would not be tolerated in modern society. We might not attempt by violent means to limit the possession of wealth, but we do recognize that the fact of possession is a great moral and political engine of power: we recognize, in a word, that the use of wealth is the real test of our civilization, and the abuse of it in self-indulgence, the corruption

*E. L. Godkin in "The Expenditures of Men of Wealth."

of justice, or the perversion of political institutions is a menace to the dearest heritage of our civil and religious life.

This sentiment must control the Christian, at least, in the use of his wealth. Although the man who acknowledges no obligation to Christ and has no spiritual ideal of life, may trust to the "note' of the age for the extent and character of his expenditures. "Sumptuous living and equipage, a coach and six maids behind," is no longer the "note" of the higher class in Europe as it was formerly. Fashion herself has decreed that the true gentleman shall have "quietness of manner, of voice, of dress, of equipage, and the vulgar ostentation of wealth shall be left to the new rich man."

Now, whether the man of the world orders his life by compulsion or willingly is a matter of no ethical moment. But with the Christian this is entirely different; the expenditure of his wealth is an integral part of his character and the administration of a sacred trust. He must follow a principle, intelligent and moral, as the expression of the ideal of his life, because his example fashions the mode, gives the tone, and animates the body politic—in a word, creates a Christian civilization, by the vitality of his spiritual ideal.

Most thinkers acknowledge that Christianity alone can save society from the destruction which certainly awaits it under a reversion to an ungenerated humanity. If the Christians of our day are to take an active and intelligent part in the work of salvation they must draw a clear, bold line of demarcation between their ideal of life and the ideal of the man of the world. In general, concerning the use and disposition of wealth there has been no such definite line and no such spiritual ideal. The Christian of to-day, in the vast majority of instances, fashions his life on an ideal which diverts the forces of wealth to the support of unfriendly and even anti-Christian objects.

In the cycle of life, as exhibited by Christian society, we see the fortunes earned by the consecrated toiler of one generation expended by the unconsecrated reveler of the next on subjects whose very names are enough to make the godly forefathers turn in their graves. It is not infrequent to see the fortune of a pious deacon, painfully earned by thrift, industry, and temperance, wasted by his descendants in the license and vice of Bohemia and the demi-monde. There must be something wrong with our ideals of life when the grandson of a Puritan scatters the accumulations of piety in the support of a Parisian actress.   This condition of things has become possible because Christians have a divided purpose in life.   They devote their hearts to the Lord, but their fortunes to their kindred, who are very often not the Lord's at all, but openly inimical to every spiritual interest sacred to the man who made the fortune.

The claims of civilization are indefinite, remote, and lack personal interest; the claims of children and relatives are definite, near and personally interesting.   The heir must be a very great rascal or the testator a very strong-minded, far-seeing man, before the fortune is directed past the tie of blood and given to philanthropic institutions.   The fruits of years of consecrated toil, the essence of this strong man's personality, the energy and virtue of a Christian life, expressing itself in the shape of accumulated wealth, may by the mere accident of fate, be lost to the cause of truth and progress, and fall into the hands of license and dishonor.

Thus the world for which Christ died, which may be reasonably represented as the world of truth, intelligence, purity, beauty, justice, honor, love—in a word a spiritual civilization—that world is not in evidence to the great mass of even professedly Christian men in the use and disposal of their wealth.   The

passion for such a civilization has never yet
taken possession of their hearts and minds.
But surely it is not impossible for the Christian
to appreciate the moral splendors of a civilization which, in our day, has called forth the
burning eloquence of poets and prophets, re-
minding us almost of the lofty strains of
Isaiah and the mystic longings of St. John—
a civilization, too, which has touched the
deepest feelings of statesmen and jurists, as
they trace the toilsome and bleeding path
along which humanity has walked to its coming hope.

Lord Charles Russell, the Chief-Justice of
England, says: "Civilization is not dominion,
wealth, material luxury; nay, not even a great
literature, and education widespread — good
though those things be. Its true signs are
thought for the poor and suffering, chivalrous
regard and respect for women, the frank recognition of human brotherhood, irrespective of
race or color, or nation or religion, the nar-
rowing of the domain of mere force as a governing factor in the world, the love of ordered
freedom, the abhorrence of what is mean and
cruel and vile, ceaseless devotion to the
claims of Justice." This definition of civilization, "the finest ever framed," is based upon
Christian truths and pervaded by the spirit of

Jesus. For such a civilization seers have dreamed their dreams and prophets have uttered their voices, martyrs have shed their blood, Apostles have toiled and spent themselves in missionary labor, saints and lovers of humanity have consecrated their lives, and we men and women of to-day, with such a glorious heritage of example behind us, must take it to a warmer place in our hearts and as the regnant principle in our spirits.

All noble Christian souls ever strive, after a sort, towards such a civilization. But like a bird with a broken wing our flight has been little better than a scurrrying run. We have risen to no majestic height secure of our own powers. Our unconsecrated wealth was our broken wing. Spiritual aims were unsupported by material forces into which the life energy of man, as long as he is on this earth, must largely pour itself. Life, divided into hostile sections, was paralyzed and a prey to destruction. The church, with a spirituality born of heaven, "has allured to better worlds" and dowered believing souls with the noblest joys of life; she has strengthened and enriched mind and heart so splendidly that the victories of both the moral and material world have rested on her banners.

How is it then that her victorious progress

is always strangely, unnaturally, illogically
arrested? She stops in her triumphant
career when she seems best fitted for further
conquest. Like an able general, vigorous in
battle but lethargic in pursuit, she has lost
the full fruits of her victory. The territory
won for Christ is constantly lost again. The
spiritual and intellectual vigor and enthusiasm
which won character, fame, and fortune seem
to decay and die in actual possession of the
fruits of the victory. Like the chiefs of some
great conqueror, Christians are virtuous, loyal,
brave, self-sacrificing in their poverty when
they have yet fortunes and honors to win,
but become cowardly, disloyal, and luxurious
when they have wealth and dukedoms to
enjoy. Among Christians, as among soldiers,
it is not enough to win and possess, nor even to
enlarge and cultivate, the personal powers in
life—a new ambition must possess the soul
thus dowered and cultivated. For the enlarged life, the new powers are not alone a new
source of enjoyment—they are an added vantage ground and a new responsibility. They
carry in themselves new laws of life and bring
with them new powers to bless and uplift in a
larger sphere, or powers of evil to spread a
wider swath of ruin and death.

For this reason the Christian man in command of resources, whether wealth, social standing, experience, intelligence, or affection, must open his heart to a new love, his spirit to a new ambition. The glory of a spiritual civilization must ravish his soul; he must come under its spell as a poet is mastered by his theme, feel its fascination as the creative artist yields to the grace of his ideal. This too, not merely because it will add zest to his own life when the world begins to pall, and active service in the ordinary routine of business has no more to offer, but because he is the divinely appointed instrument for the accomplishment of this great purpose of redemption. He is false to God and to humanity who locks up the treasures of education, experience, wealth, in his own heart when the bleeding world is calling for their saving ministry.

Moreover if the Gospel can save men, inspire the soul, enlarge the mind, enrich the spirit, and give life so many successes, so that a Christian man is the full-orbed, normal, and complete man, but when this masterpiece is finished there is no field for the exercise of those rich, large, gracious powers, then is the Gospel but a more disastrous failure as an instrument for the sublimer end of a spiritual civilization. It is a torso, not a perfected statue, and the eye of humanity looks with longing at those noble lines which prophesy the glory which might have been. We trust to see the dawning of a new day in the increasing instances of men and women of the most richly endowed natures and the most brilliantly successful professional and commercial careers recognizing their duty to society and passionately accepting, with the spirit of the old Confessors, the way of the new service and the ideal of the new civilization.

Such an instance is that of John Ruskin: "Refusing the invitations of the rich and putting away the temptation to a life of elegant ease and refined luxury, he gave himself to the poor. His best lectures were never given where English wealth and social prestige were represented, but were delivered to working girls' clubs and workingmen's associations. If Rousseau refused the yoke of law and service upon the plea of genius, this man, by reason of his talents, was careful to fulfil the duties not expected of mediocrity. No man has done so much to lift the veil which hides the grim realities of poverty from the gay dreams of wealth. By his life and example Ruskin has earned the right to speak as a prophet to those who stand upon the threshold of the nineteenth century."*

* N. D. Hillis, D. D., Sermon on John Ruskin.

If then we can read the economic lesson of the centuries that "Savage nations are always poor," and if we can perceive the great spiritual truth concerning wealth, that "It is a divinely ordained instrument for promoting the highest Christian civilization," we shall have discovered the essential truths which furnish the Christian who has accumulated wealth a just principle for its administration in the interests of the Kingdom of Christ Jesus. In this case he will perceive it to be a power spiritual of which he is possessor and a sacred trust of which he is the divinely appointed trustee; and from these obligations to his own soul, to his fellow-men, and to God there is no discharge. If Christianity is to be saved from eating out its own heart, and vindicated as the supernatural regenerator of society, Christians must loyally accept the principle of increasing obligation with the possession of increasing resources. So will society, as well as souls, become the subject of its redemptive agencies.

Christianity is being tested now as never before in the history of the world — not by external enemies, but by lofty ideas and principles of action which she herself has done most to call into existence. Can she rise to the demand of the hour? Can she answer those calls of the Holy Spirit, which, like the

Word of God, "pierces to the dividing of both soul and spirit, and is quick to discern the thoughts and intents of the heart" ? Are the followers of Jesus in the last decade of the nineteenth century able to submit their life to the dominion of this lofty and heroic ideal?

Under it a new career of service and honor awaits all strong, resourceful souls; there will be new worlds to conquer, larger plans of work, deeper draughts of pleasure. Character would be identified with such an administration of wealth and such a use of power; nobleness and social distinction would be inseparable from such service; it would be at once a test of loyalty to Christ and loyalty to the Nation. It would be a sure indication of that passion for righteousness in the life of nations which burns up the baser elements in souls and sets free the pure metal of a redeemed life to enrich society with the treasures of heaven. Under its refining fires we should see the church of Christ glow with the primal purity of the Apostolic days; its divine breath would inspire her for a new mission, its moral energy would arm her for a new conquest. Disciplined by its high demands she would emerge " fair as the moon, clear as the sun, and terrible as an army with banners."

XVIII.

THE SCOPE AND SANITY OF THE NEW IDEAL.

The intelligent reader of these pages will readily perceive that no appeal has been made to passion and hardly any to mere sentiment. Our aim has been to present the sanity and sweet reasonableness of the doctrine that wealth is a trust, and that its wise and Christian administration demands the exercise of the noblest religious character and the rarest civic spirit. Our care has been to avoid all those violent class prejudices often allowed to poison the mind and to keep clear of demagogic harangues so often served up, instead of argument, in the attempt to array the poor against the rich. No subject is so delicate of adjustment, none so difficult to understand and apply safely to the complex realities of life, as the relation of Christianity to wealth. Yet concerning no other have so much foolishness, violence, and crudity been spoken and written.

Some social reformers can see nothing but one side of the subject; they will listen to no considerations that have weighed with men in the past, and predict nothing but disaster unless the economic foundations are destroyed and a new society created on principles diametrically opposed to and essentially contradictory of the business and social life which now obtains. But a subject so vast, delicate, and radical as this cannot be understood without patient study; it can not be settled by appeals to feeling; it must gain the reason and intelligence as well as the affections and the will.

The Christian man in possession of accumulated wealth, when asked to change his ideal of life for the express purpose of affecting the use of his money, is bound by the strongest obligations to himself and society to ascertain clearly the scope and meaning of the new ideal. He must assure himself that such a proposal will not bring down upon his own head a greater disaster than the danger he is trying to prevent; he must look into the future if he may discern the fate of society as it would be affected by these new social and economic principles. He can thus urge, in the interests of caution, the very obligations of wealth which the social reformer urges in support of the economic revolution. Moreover, the persons for whom these considerations are especially intended are, in most instances, careful, experienced, wise, perhaps even shrewd, men of business who have accumulated or retained wealth, and by virtue of this fact are not subjects upon whom the dreams of socialists or the raving of fanatics are likely to produce much effect. But they are Christians, presumably open to consider the reasonable moral obligations which wealth entails, and susceptible to the spiritual ideals of life which lie at the basis of all really Christian society, and must inspire every method for the higher uses of wealth.

We desire in a few sentences to show, the leading human interests involved in this discussion, and see how they would be affected, and thus, with our eyes open to the sacred possibilities of life and our wills in generous surrender to the new truths of the Gospel, we may open our hearts to the best influences of our age and manifest in our lives the noble and gracious principles of the teaching and practice of our Lord Jesus Christ.

The broad issue, as stated, is between our Christian selfhood and the claims of society. Are they antagonistic or complementary? Is the modern doctrine of the solidarity of the race and the claims of society upon the believer a denial of the hitherto accepted doctrine of individualism? The question involves the

fundamental doctrines both of religion and society. On its threshold we are met by the
claims of personality—the individual's rights
to the development, exercise, enjoyment,
and fruits of his own powers, physical, intellectual, and spiritual. If we deny these
to the Christian man we attack the doctrine of
personality in Christ and in God. Such a
denial would logically lead us to the waste
desolation of Buddhistic nothingness and eternal night. The horror and despair of pantheistic
pessimism, that life itself is a mistake and con-
sciousness a curse—yawn before us in that dark
gulf. Against the black horror of this atheistic denial of the good of life and the glory of
salvation I, as a redeemed soul, enfranchised,
crowned with a noble selfhood in Christ, assert
myself. The Christian possesses a selfhood
which carries with its redemption every prerogative of personality and manhood into the
new life of the spirit. Thus I stand in the
presence of the eternal realities of God, of the
Holy Spirit, of the Christ, and of the Human
Soul. Here Christianity is positive, assertive,
vital, and aggressive.

But these are certainly not theological ab-
stractions: they are historical realities or mani-
festations of life which bear upon the concrete
facts of existence; they live, think, work, suf-

fer, and triumph in this present physical life; and touch our present interest, in asserting the positive possession of property. It is not difficult to see, therefore, why all anarchistic and atheistic systems have attacked the principle of the personal possession of property. The right to own property is simply the material symbol of the right to exist, to know, to believe, to enjoy, to love, to serve, to reign. It involves not only man's right, but Christ's and God's. The creator's possessions are material as well as spiritual: "The cattle on a thousand hills are mine," "The silver and the gold are mine," is the assertion of Him who also claims the allegiance of our spirits and whose riches are souls.

We have maintained as a fundamental principle of religion, of society, and of human personality, that the Christian man has a right to own property; and with this right follows its control, disposal, and varied administration, subject only to the law of God. All schemes, expedients, plans, and laws which touch this right are essentially anarchistic and destructive at once of Christianity and human society. The only considerations that can be allowed to modify this right are such as grow out of the right itself. Thus, the strength of our reasoning concerning the administration of wealth lies in the doctrine of Christian selfhood and the right of personal possessions which it carries with it.

Therefore the obligation to use wealth wisely and for the higher spiritual ends of life is not blackmail paid to society in order that the remainder may be used for personal gratification. Possession always involves use, and use is either wise or unwise—it either blesses or bans; it reaches inwardly to the possessor, and outwardly to society. To regard wealth as a trust, and to administer it in the interests of society, is not, however, a denial of the principle of possession nor a limitation of, nor a concession of weakness in that principle; it is simply a perception of its higher ends and uses, and an acknowledgment that it is abused when used only for personal gratification, and that spiritual service for one's self and society are the greatest advantges of fortune. For this reason the effects of such a use of wealth must ever be personal. In the close and immediate sense of promoting the culture, and strength of one's own intellectual and spiritual nature, as well as furnishing the stage of action for enlarged service in the industrial and moral life of society its benefits are personal.

Thus, and thus only, does wealth purchase for its owner all that is potential in it. The

socialist and unfriendly critic may point out
that Christianity has existed now for nearly
two thousand years, and not yet created such
an ideal use of wealth, either for the owners
themselves or for use in society. We
acknowledge and lament the fact that human
nature is so slow in the larger spiritual appre-
hensions; but Christianity is not by any means
alone in this peculiarity of our defective intellectual and spiritual development.

Science was as long about the perception of
the Creator's thoughts in nature as religion
was about his thoughts in scripture and society. It is but of yesterday that Newton,
Laplace, Faraday, Tyndale, and Thomson revealed the secrets of Nature. Nature has
been before us these thousands of years an
open book, but we had no key to her language.
It is far more strange that her interpretation
should have been so long delayed than that
selfish, prejudiced, human hearts, even after
they have come under the teachings of the
Holy Spirit, should be so slow to learn those
difficult lessons concerning wealth, which not
only require a clear head, but a surrendered
will and a pure heart. This is indeed the feature of the new ideal of life which indicates its
true character and far-reaching influence.

It is not an intellectual proposition which

may be demonstrated by a process of reasoning, and so left secure of its own application because proved. It has not only to be understood, but accepted, submitted to, and loved. It is at once an ideal which appeals to the most spiritual qualities of our Christian manhood and a practical plan of life which penetrates and rules among the details of our material existence. It reaches from the temple to the kitchen, from the university to the workshop, and affects our most exalted mood and most sordid cares. It goes beyond the individual to the family. It requires the exercise of the free will, and it lays its strong hand upon heredity and race. It reverses largely the principle upon which modern society has built up family fortunes and names, and it demands strict personal service before it will yield a better social life. It lays its strong hand upon the man's business, and it modifies his conceptions of fame, comfort, and pleasure.

It is impossible that such an ideal could have gained large credence, not to say acceptance, under the conditions which Christianity has had to pass through in its checkered history. For many hundreds of years European Christianity had to struggle for its very existence; and after external enemies were overcome it still had to grope blindly, often amid tears and blood, after the meaning of its own leading truths, so slow of apprehension and so hard of acceptance are the vital ideas that determine the destiny of races and the form of civilized society.

Furthermore we are dealing with a principle of human conduct which requires a complementary knowledge of material things and of human history, as well as the precepts of divine revelation. The Christian church had to find out, by a slow, hard experience, what wealth is, how it is produced, what laws govern its use and possession, and what relation it bears to the civil and moral life of the people, before she could begin to see its bearing upon great Christian ideals of society and the Kingdom of God.

It is very significant, that popular liberty, and indeed all human progress, has been inseparably associated with the question of taxes. Nations and kings have both known that the concentrated energy of a people stored up in the treasury of the State largely determines the matter of autocracy or freedom, of the decay or permanence of governments. These struggles in politics, social life, and physical nature had to arrive at some quality of definiteness, and come into contact with the matured thought of Christianity about itself, before the relation of wealth and Christianity could be clearly seen and strongly felt. Here and there, it is true, gifted individuals were enlightened on such a theme, as the summits of the Alps catch the rosy colors of the morning long before the valleys are yellow with the light of the sun. But we are treating of a principle which governs nations and civilizations—a method of action which is of universal social application, not the rapt vision vouchsafed to solitary, far-seeing souls. It is not strange, therefore, that we have been so long in understanding this claim of the higher life, for the data from which alone we could reason have but recently been gathered from the facts of life around us.

Again the century which has seen the greatest progress in political liberty, in scientific research, and consequently in the accumulation of material wealth, has also witnessed the clearest recognition of this principle of obligation in the expenditure of wealth. In one sense, the one is an accompaniment of the other, but that does not alter the fact, historically considered, that the obligation could never have been perceived in all its scope and felt in all its power without those previous achievements in civil life and those discoveries in science, combined with new ideals in religion   Indeed, we are face to face with a new epoch, we are entering a new era of social development; not because one particular truth hitherto unheard of in the church and the State is now discovered for the first time, and being made the battle cry of the reformers, but because mutually helpful and complementary truths, hitherto divorced and unfriendly, are being accepted as mutually explanatory and necessary parts of a great whole.

Selfhood, which is the right to possess and enjoy with its corresponding obligation to social service, is seen to be, both in grace and nature, the only foundation of civilized society. The fair blossom of family life springs from the vital seed of personality.   The glorious tree of Christian civilization with all its precious fruits of art, literature, science, education and soul culture, strikes its tap-root deep in the rich soil of a regenerated selfhood.

This new ideal of the Christian life is not the monopoly of a class, but the heritage of all men; this is no Utopian dream, but the reasoned result of civil and religious truth; this needs no appeal to fanaticism for acceptance or denial, it just comes, like the dawn, into the open window of every receptive soul. We have advanced so far on the road of progress it is impossible to go back; all great hearts who feel the people's sorrows, and all noble souls who hear their Divine leader's call, will advance, carrying the improved weapon and keeping step to the thrilling music of the new age.

How then shall we choose to live during those opening years of the new century—the new millennium — under the strong, clear, steady light which the age has brought us concerning the totality of our life and duty? If it were a purely economic subject like the production and distribution of wealth, it could be safely relegated by us to experts in political economy and to the general principles of honesty and self-interest in commerce. But the new relations of Christian personality to wealth teach us that the production, distribution, and use of wealth is a moral and spiritual question, an obligation bearing upon our most inward character, and reaching out to society and downward through civilized community life for countless generations.

Peace and War, Life and Death, seem standing around in suspense waiting for the momentous decision of the Christian church as to how her members will discharge the obligations of the new era. This problem cannot be solved by artificial attempts to get rid of our wealth. This would be seeking refuge in the old idea of denial and lead us back to savagery and night. If our education, skill, and virtue create wealth in all civilized communities, its possession is a condition of Christian civilized life. We must live in the atmosphere which such powers and virtues have created. We might cut the gordian knot by rising out of this atmosphere, as the aëronaut throws over his ballast, but only to suffer asphyxia or to be frozen to death.

The Christian problem of our day is harder, because it carries with it the moral and spiritual fate of individuals and society. It is harder, because to use and expend is always harder than to earn and gather; because it is always harder to live than to die. It is harder, because it is more difficult to walk in the golden medium than to be a fanatic in religion, or a rake and worldling. Christianity has had a large complement of followers, devoted, holy, intense, spiritual souls, who have despised the world, risen victorious over its allurements, counted life itself as nothing before the prize of glory in their ecstatic vision, and from thrones of power have stepped aside into the cell of poverty. She has had assertive natures also,—soldiers, statesmen, merchants, scholars, men who have led the van of progress and gathered riches and power and

honor. But she has had few who have combined these features of life—few who as workers and fighters have seen the spiritual potency
of wealth and power in combination with
purity of heart, tenderness of spirit, and ideals
of brotherhood; few who as thinkers and saints
have seen the material creations of the spirit
in combination with industry, thrift, courage,
hope, and a civic loyalty.

The task of Christian thinkers to-day is
to combine these hitherto separated ideals of
life. We must find a principle of action
which counts business as holy as worship, indeed as itself a worship in the spirit of brotherhood and help which all true business implies. A principle of life which holds the
forum as sacred as the temple and the workshop as holy as the altar, which treats the
physical needs of men as tenderly and sacredly
as their spiritual weaknesses, and which draws
no line of demarcation between sacred and
secular. A principle which leads us to a genuine imitation of Christ in making all life
sacred, all service a doing of "the Father's
business." A principle, finally, which creates
no gulf of separation between a man's private
character and his public conduct, which will
make impossible the self-deception of the man
who, intent on private virtues, is yet recreant

to public obligations; which, in a word, teaches a man to see in the face of society the reflex of his own character, and will use every resource of brain and heart, of spirit and means, to change that image both in himself and in society into the image of Jesus Christ.

That principle, applicable to every age and condition of life, is that wealth (resources of every kind—brains, affection, experience), is a trust, and that the administration of such a trust is the most sacred duty, the holiest obligation of the Christian man; that the fate of the individual and the fate of society, the future of children, and the success of religion are dependent upon the manner in which this obligation is met.

This principle builds upon the past experience of the race like all sane, safe proposals for human betterment, yet it listens to the truth of the present like all true prophets of God. It treasures the concentrated wisdom of teachers, the example of heroes, and the devotion of saints who have served God well in their time, and makes no break in the splendid tradition of noble lives whose names are still an inspiration to the believer. But it reads their story to mean that if we would follow in their footsteps we must learn the new lessons, solve the new problems, rise to the new duties, and

enlist for the new service to which the voice
of Christ plainly calls us.

This sane and balanced judgment gives it
life and the promise of future power, as the
recipient of the living spirit of God, teaching us the truths of our own age and help-
ing us to quit us like men. It demands,
undoubtedly, a high type of Christian intelligence and morality; but surely, after nearly
two thousand years of teaching and example,
the Christian church can furnish that to her ad-
herents. It demands somewhat of an acknowledgment of failure, and even gross errors,
selfishness, and slowness of understanding in
the past, but shall Christians take refuge in
pride and self-sufficiency, rather than humility
and repentance? It summons us to a high
and serene consideration of the issues of human life, speaks to us in a language which to
many yet is strange, unreal, and idealistic, and
seems to bid us act in a world of dreams.
But these divine dreams may be the grandest
realities; for how many of those gracious
teachings on the slopes of Galilee, read in the
cold, hard, materialistic light of our worldly
aims, seem dreams, seen as it were by eyes of
another kind from ours? Yet those dreams
were made splendid realities by men and women whose great faith and great souls enabled

them to enter into the fellowship of Christ's truth and service and suffering. And out of those eternal and spiritual realities of his teaching, who was to the world but a dreamer and defeated man, were born the moral purity, intellectual vitality, social and family affection, and spirit of liberty, which saved Europe from corruption, despair, and anarchy. Out of these things have sprung the new manhood and womanhood, the love of ordered freedom, and the Kingdom of God which is to-day the refuge and hope of all despairing as well as aspiring souls.

Therefore let not the practical man of the world despise our dreams: in his heart of hearts he longs for their realization; in the dreary prosaic monotony of his life they are the promise of color and music and grace and sweetness, entering into his soul to lead him up to the threshold of heaven. Let him enter there through the blood of Christ, and learn for himself the meaning of the dream.

We shall come under the guidance of this principle, to a new dispensation of the spirit which consecrates all material things, as if the Divine Master said to us anew "Gather up the fragments that nothing be lost." Has the church not lost for the material comfort of life much of the resources which her Divine Head created by His power over the physical conditions of life? Led by the teaching of such a truth we shall feel new tenderness and sympathy for every form of human suffering and sorrow, and new sacredness for every form of human life, whether rich or poor. It will create an intimacy and friendship, unknown before, between the sordid drudgery and toil of the laborer and the lofty aspirations of the seer, between the cold calculations of the man of business and the devout enthusiasm of the saint. Nay, this shall help to rob the toil of its sordidness and give it spiritual dignity; it shall bring into business the holy warmth of a serving son of God. This principle of life shall be a new spirit moving in the common ways of men, like Jesus among his contemporaries, "familiar, condescending, free," yet opening our eyes to the rich and splendid visions which bring the poetry of great and gifted souls into common clay.

Now this divine fabric of the new social order is reared on the firm foundation of the physical nature around us, on the family life, the home, the school, the common ways of trade and art and science and music and literature. It demands for its realization no fanatical or impossible vagary of the intellect or spirit, no violence to the elemental and normal powers of the body or the soul. It will come into our homes a wise, gracious friend; it will nourish our kindred with its love, and adorn our life with taste and refinement. It threatens no revolution nor destruction of interests which religion and nature both tell us should ever be sacred. It sets no bounds to progress, but rather promises, with the accession of a new vital force, a renascence of creative power in every department of human activity. It has all the marks of a natural, inevitable, and resistless movement of the mind and spirit.

Every candid man we hopefully believe, desires its realization, and we only regret that our weakness and selfishness may hinder its sway over all our life. We feel its breath upon our fevered temples as the hope of immortality came to the jaded, skeptical Roman world in the days of Christ. We, too, are in the exhausted period that precedes transition into a stronger, nobler life. We have lost many things, and others still have lost their definiteness of outline, their power of carrying conviction to our minds and fascination over our hearts. We do not believe and love as men who live near Nature and close to the heart of humanity, men who honor great deeds and suffer in silence, for these traits are becoming rarer among us.

Yet more in practical life the acceptance of this obligation would be a new vow of obedience to the simple teachings of Jesus, a new imitation of His example and a new inspiration of His spirit. It would renew in our life the simplicity of faith and the clearness of truth, for we should know of the doctrine by His own plan of doing His will. We should renew our hopes, possess again the joy of fellowship, and have the conscious dignity of walking with God. In comparison with this renewal of all the vital forces of the soul and all these saving influences on society, how mean and contemptible are the gratifications and ambitions of unconsecrated wealth.

The Christian man who, in these latter days, shall grow up into the stature of perfect manhood in Christ Jesus is one who shall consecrate all the resources of a strong, wise, regenerated nature, and lay all its success, material and moral, on the altar of service for his fellow-men. Such an one will hear his Master say "Inasmuch as ye have done it unto the least of these my brethren, ye have done it unto me." He may look into the faces of his own children and lovingly say "I have done the best for them," and they will rise up and call him blessed. He may look out upon the public life, and hear "the blessing of him that was ready to perish" mingle with the music of the rich, strong voice of the new civilization, which he has helped largely to create. Thus in the possession of a Christian selfhood, which is the richest form of personality, and in the noble and inspiring activities of personal service, which is the only social virtue, he will attain, the highest crown of all redeemed souls—a holy kinship with the Elder Brother. He alone can truly teach him the sacredness and strength of those ideals of life and bonds of brotherhood which alone can sustain the splendid fabric of a Christian society and usher happy hearts into the Kingdom of God.

PRINTED BY R. R. DONNELLEY
AND SONS CO. AT THE LAKESIDE
PRESS, CHICAGO, MDCCCXCVIII

Trieste

Trieste Publishing has a massive catalogue of classic book titles. Our aim is to provide readers with the highest quality reproductions of fiction and non-fiction literature that has stood the test of time. The many thousands of books in our collection have been sourced from libraries and private collections around the world.

The titles that Trieste Publishing has chosen to be part of the collection have been scanned to simulate the original. Our readers see the books the same way that their first readers did decades or a hundred or more years ago. Books from that period are often spoiled by imperfections that did not exist in the original. Imperfections could be in the form of blurred text, photographs, or missing pages. It is highly unlikely that this would occur with one of our books. Our extensive quality control ensures that the readers of Trieste Publishing's books will be delighted with their purchase. Our staff has thoroughly reviewed every page of all the books in the collection, repairing, or if necessary, rejecting titles that are not of the highest quality. This process ensures that the reader of one of Trieste Publishing's titles receives a volume that faithfully reproduces the original, and to the maximum degree possible, gives them the experience of owning the original work.

We pride ourselves on not only creating a pathway to an extensive reservoir of books of the finest quality, but also providing value to every one of our readers. Generally, Trieste books are purchased singly - on demand, however they may also be purchased in bulk. Readers interested in bulk purchases are invited to contact us directly to enquire about our tailored bulk rates. Email: customerservice@triestepublishing.com

You May Also Like

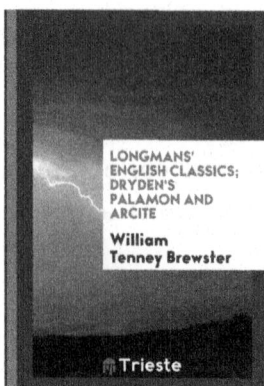

Longmans' English Classics; Dryden's Palamon and Arcite

William Tenney Brewster

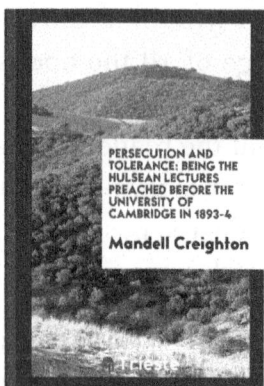

ISBN: 9780649565733
Paperback: 170 pages
Dimensions: 6.14 x 0.36 x 9.21 inches
Language: eng

Persecution and Tolerance: Being the Hulsean Lectures Preached Before the University of Cambridge in 1893-4

Mandell Creighton

ISBN: 9780649669356
Paperback: 164 pages
Dimensions: 6.14 x 0.35 x 9.21 inches
Language: eng

www.triestepublishing.com

You May Also Like

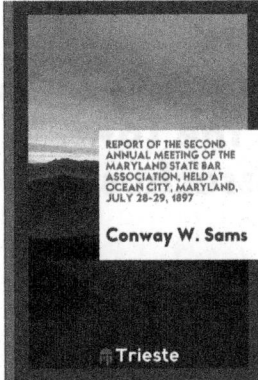

Report of the Second Annual Meeting of the Maryland State Bar Association, Held at Ocean City, Maryland, July 28-29, 1897

Conway W. Sams

ISBN: 9780649724185
Paperback: 130 pages
Dimensions: 6.14 x 0.28 x 9.21 inches
Language: eng

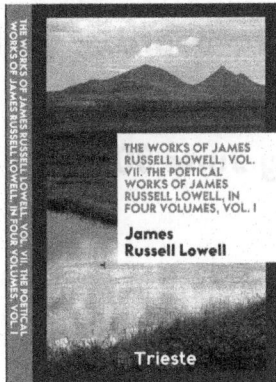

The Works of James Russell Lowell, Vol. VII. The Poetical Works of James Russell Lowell, in Four Volumes, Vol. I

James Russell Lowell

ISBN: 9780649640430
Paperback: 332 pages
Dimensions: 6.14 x 0.69 x 9.21 inches
Language: eng

You May Also Like

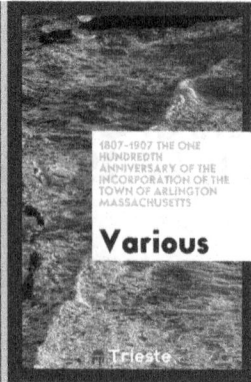

1807-1907 The One Hundredth Anniversary of the incorporation of the Town of Arlington Massachusetts

Various

ISBN: 9780649420544
Paperback: 108 pages
Dimensions: 6.14 x 0.22 x 9.21 inches
Language: eng

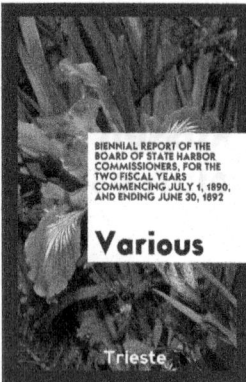

Biennial report of the Board of State Harbor Commissioners, for the two fiscal years commencing July 1, 1890, and ending June 30, 1892

Various

ISBN: 9780649194292
Paperback: 44 pages
Dimensions: 6.14 x 0.09 x 9.21 inches
Language: eng

You May Also Like

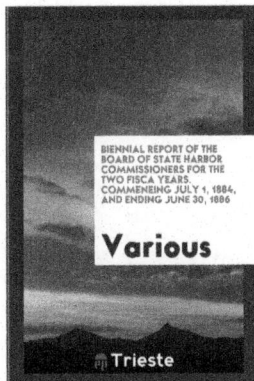

Biennial report of the Board of State Harbor Commissioners for the two fisca years. Commeneing July 1, 1884, and Ending June 30, 1886

Various

ISBN: 9780649199693
Paperback: 48 pages
Dimensions: 6.14 x 0.10 x 9.21 inches
Language: eng

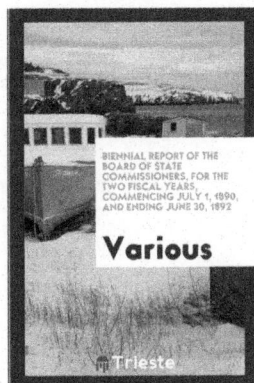

Biennial report of the Board of state commissioners, for the two fiscal years, commencing July 1, 1890, and ending June 30, 1892

Various

ISBN: 9780649196395
Paperback: 44 pages
Dimensions: 6.14 x 0.09 x 9.21 inches
Language: eng

Find more of our titles on our website. We have a selection of thousands of titles that will interest you. Please visit

www.triestepublishing.com

Lightning Source UK Ltd.
Milton Keynes UK
UKOW01f1021231017
311488UK00009B/2646/P

9 780649 701551